P9-APC-695

TELL STORIES

GET HIRED

INNOVATIVE STRATEGIES

TO LAND YOUR NEXT JOB AND ADVANCE YOUR CAREER

To Mahomed
From Daisy
Best wishes as you embark
on your new life in Canada!

DAISY WRIGHT

This book, in most cases, uses English, not American, spelling, so don't be surprised to see acknowledgement instead of acknowledgment, colour instead of color, behaviour instead of behavior, or judgement instead of judgment. These spellings should in no way detract from the meaning of the content.

Printed in the USA

For information on book purchases please write:
WCS Publishers,
164 Sandalwood Parkway East,
Suite 211, P.O. Box 1026,
Brampton, ON,
L6Z 4X1

Book design by Maureen Cutajar
www.gopublished.com

Library and Archives Canada Cataloguing in Publication

Wright, Daisy, author
Tell stories, get hired : innovative strategies to land your next job and advance your career / Daisy Wright ; Angela J. Carter, editor.

Includes bibliographical references.
ISBN 978-0-9813104-4-2 (pbk.)

1. Job hunting--Handbooks, manuals, etc. 2. Career development--Handbooks, manuals, etc. I. Carter, Angela J., editor II. Title.

HF5382.7.W75 2014 650.14 C2014-904366-X

This book is dedicated to the many people I have had the privilege of helping with their career transitions. You have inspired me to become a better career development practitioner.

It's also dedicated to you, as you begin your new journey to career success.

Acknowledgements

It took a village to write this book, and I couldn't have done it without the support, participation, collaboration and generosity of many, many people. I appreciate and thank all the contributors for the immense value they have added to **Tell Stories, Get Hired.** Without your contributions, there wouldn't have been a book of this calibre.

I also appreciate and thank:

- My immediate family – husband (Patrick), daughter (Damali), and son (Guion). Thank you all for, once again, putting up with me on another book project.
- Six-year old grandson Dakari, whose uninvited entry into my office forced me many times to take a break, but more importantly, whose faith is stronger than mine. Let me illustrate this briefly. At age five, he and his mom got stuck in the snow while she was taking him to school. After they became unstuck, he said to her, "Mom, when next you get stuck, ask Jesus for help." What wise words? In the world of job search and career advancement, don't we get stuck all the time? We can't do it by ourselves, and so we need to seek the help of a higher power! Dakari, you are Grandma's little Blessing, and I love you!
- My other family members for their constant support. You are too numerous to mention here, but you know who you are, and I thank you all for being family.
- My niece Donnadene's husband, Denver Jeffrey, whose untimely passing interrupted the project in its final stage. I pay tribute to

him here, not only because his life exemplified someone who told his stories to get hired, but he was a champion for developing people. Those were the sentiments expressed by his former colleagues and direct reports at the County Hall Marriott and Sopwell House Hotels in London, England. His legacy will continue in the lives of his daughters, Danielle & Dilanna.

- Angela Carter, editor and friend, whose invaluable assistance helped to make the content flow as best as possible. You are a true champion.
- Lynda Reeves, Paul Copcutt and Cecile Peterkin. While you did not contribute directly to this book, as original contributors to **No Canadian Experience, Eh?** I drew on your expertise to rewrite sections under references, personal branding, social media, and onboarding.
- My friends Norma Hodgson, Maureen Maragh and Sandy Richards for your special prayers and spiritual conversations during my many start and stop moments.
- Franne McNeal, Jane Harnadek, Mark Anthony Dyson and Lita Pitruzzello, for your support and encouragement.
- The generous individuals who made up Career Professionals of Canada Entrepreneurs' Master Mind Group. Our monthly calls always brought a fresh approach to how to do our job more effectively.
- David Perry, author and executive search extraordinaire, for agreeing to be interviewed, as well as for his support over the years.
- Career Catalyst, Phyllis Mufson, who helps job seekers make their dreams a reachable reality, and who has been a one of my main supporters.
- Recruiter, Speaker, & Career Consultant, Abby Kohut, who has inspired me with her Job Search Success Tour to educate one million job seekers across the USA.
- Mark Babbitt and Mack Watts of YouTern for sharing my job search blog posts when they can.

- The twenty-three women who participated in the six-week Daniel Plan Program at Bramalea Free Methodist Church. Space would not permit me to list your names, but your presence each week demonstrated a commitment that every job seeker should emulate.

This Acknowledgement list would not be complete if I didn't mention two groups on Twitter from which I have gain knowledge and inspiration.

- The #TChat Community, also known as @TalentCulture. This is a weeklyTwitter Chat where professional peers in human resources and recruiting, talk about issues that affect the "world of work". It is a place where career practitioners and job seekers can contribute and learn from experts.
- The #WHYiGIVE Community, another weekly Twitter Chat where people celebrate generosity. It not only provides a respite from my writing and research, but provides spiritual inspiration to keep me going. This community is huge, but I want to thank @michaelchatman, host of the #WHYiGIVEChat, and contributors, @pamfong7, @thewarford, @foulksd and @AM_Morgan. You all inspire me by your philanthropic work and engaging spirit.

Foreword

As the founder of *Career Professionals of Canada*, a national association for career practitioners, I have made it my life's work to empower people to succeed in their career. I have always been fascinated by the power of career storytelling, so when Daisy Wright mentioned that she was writing a book to help jobseekers learn and apply this technique, I was overjoyed. Having had the pleasure of presenting Daisy with the prestigious *Outstanding Canadian Career Leader Award* for her work in our field, I am delighted to write this foreword.

It's a *fact of life*: The candidate who best sells his or her value to the hiring authority gets the job.

When it comes to job search, we cannot underestimate the importance of storytelling. If you can articulate your value effectively, you can succeed in your job search. Career storytelling can help you build credibility, but its benefits don't end there. It can also help you to identify your dreams, strengthen your values, find your true assets, and build your self-confidence.

Our current job search environment is very competitive and the only way to differentiate yourself is to tell "signature stories." Throughout this book, Daisy shares many tips, techniques, and tools to help you uncover the many accomplishments in your career and shape them into a fascinating story.

Every career has many interesting *twists and turns*, but few people are naturally confident storytellers. Most people find the thought of having to "sell" themselves to recruiters, hiring managers, and other potential company representatives daunting. You may know what you want to share, but are not certain of how best to do that. Daisy reveals ways to develop and communicate your value proposition and personal brand, and gives tactical steps to enhancing your social profile – both online and in person.

You'll learn networking strategies and new ways to build meaningful relationships. By applying the basics such as "body language," you'll find that you can engage recruiters, employers, and other colleagues. After learning the intricacies of elevator speeches and interview scripts, you'll soon be connecting more effectively with other people in the workplace and benefitting from references, mentors, and sponsors.

Daisy has a way of bringing together some of the leading minds in career development. The list of contributing experts that share their own stories is a global "who's who" in the field. Leveraging their combined expertise, she has compiled leading-edge resources to help you. Throughout, you'll find numerous examples that you can use for inspiration in developing your own career stories.

Most job seekers struggle with selecting and narrating stories for career documents. Your self-marketing documents, including your résumé, cover letter, biography, and job proposal, should tell your stories effectively. Condensing your accomplishments into a few short bullet points need not be frustrating. Through *Tell Stories, Get Hired*, you'll learn how to explain your career achievements clearly and concisely.

We tell stories every day, but we rarely have to do so in a stressful job search environment. It's one thing to be the person asking questions in a job interview – but it's completely different when you are being asked the questions. If you are the least bit anxious about interviews, you will find this book transformative. You'll learn how to conquer your fears and bounce back from difficult career situations. Most of all, you will ensure that you stay authentic and tell your stories with honesty. Once you are onboard in your new job, you'll be able to maintain that integrity.

I met Daisy early in my own career, while I was running one of Canada's top executive résumé services. We hit it off right away. It seemed that we had much in common – we were captivated by our clients' stories and passionate about helping them tell those stories effectively.

Over the years, I have watched Daisy build her own career while her focus has evolved from helping new entrants to the market and new immigrants to enabling supervisors, managers, and emerging executives achieve career success through storytelling.

It's not surprising that Daisy loves having conversations with her clients, uncovering their success stories, and arming them with an achievement-rich résumé. Through storytelling, Daisy assists individuals in career transition to clarify their career path, improve their employability, and enhance their self-esteem. Once her work is complete, she stands back as they walk confidently into networking meetings, interviews, and ultimately their new careers.

With Daisy's complete dedication and focus on her clients, she has often expressed that one of her most enjoyable experiences is receiving a call back from a client to hear that they have achieved their goal!

What I can tell you about Daisy is that she is genuine. With a career built on effective communication, Daisy herself is a great storyteller.

Her own career is rich and full – replete with client successes. The stories she tells are realistic and helpful. Over the years, I have enjoyed listening to her seminars, workshops, and keynote presentations.

Watching Daisy's career evolve has been more than energizing. Her story has evolved once again as she is now one of my closest advisors on the board of *Career Professionals of Canada*.

Reading this book has been a pleasure. Enjoy all the insights and apply them to your next job search!

—Sharon Graham, Canada's Career Strategist

Author of the *Best Canadian Résumés Series* and *The Canadian Career Strategist Series*

Founder and executive director of *Career Professionals of Canada*

Panel of Contributing Experts

I would like to introduce you to some contributing experts who have either offered strategies on how to tell stories to get hired, or have shared their stories on how they got hired. Some have even hired themselves, when they came up against one obstacle after the other. They are from Canada, the United States and as far away as the United Kingdom and France, and their experiences are just as diverse. One thing they all have in common is a desire to see individuals succeed using their innate talents.

They are:

- Arie Ball, Vice President, Talent Acquisition, Sodexo
- Audrey Prenzel, Founder, Résumé Resources
- Carole Martin, President, Interview Coach
- Christine Brown-Quinn & Jacqueline Frost, Co-founders and managing directors of the virtual Women in Business Superseries, focusing on career development
- Guillermo Ziegler, Software Testing Professional
- Jenn Harris, CEO, High Heel Golfer
- John Ribeiro, Manager, Process Automation, Rogers Communications Inc.
- Julie Smith, Founder, Success Through Stillness Approach and Peaceful Sleep System
- Kimberly Robb Baker, Chief Career Storyteller, Movin' On Up Résumés

- Lauren Holliday, Journalist and Full-Stack Marketer
- Lori-Anne Fitzpatrick, Director, Business Performance, Rogers Communications Inc.
- Marguerite Orane, Founder and CEO, Marguerite Orane & Associates
- Maureen McCann, Chief Career Strategist and Owner, ProMotion Career Solutions
- Rajni Dogra (Dr.), Professor, Economics, Sheridan College
- Razwana Wahid, Owner and Writer, Your Work Is Your Life
- Stephen Hinton, President, Hinton Human Capital
- Sue Edwards, President, Development By Design
- Sukhjit Singh, Employment Counsellor
- Wayne Pagani, Owner/Principal Consultant, W. P. Consulting

Contents

Introduction

> *I believe that within each person lies a story. A story that can inspire, teach, excite, or motivate. It can change people's lives.*
>
> ~ Brian Tracy

A few years ago, I wrote a magazine article about behavioural interviewing titled **Tell Stories, Get Hired.** Since then, I have realized that storytelling has not only become a central theme to the job search process, but also a powerful way to communicate in any setting. It doesn't matter what you are engaged in – an interview, a networking event, delivering an elevator speech, participating in meetings, communicating one-on-one, or creating job search documents – it is imperative that you learn how to tell stories that will communicate value and build credibility.

In his book, **Tell to Win**, Peter Gruber states: "Today everyone – whether they know it or not – is in the **emotional transportation business**. More and more, success is won by creating **compelling stories** that have the power to move partners, shareholders, customers and employees to action. Simply put, if you can't tell it, you can't sell it." As a job seeker, if you can't engage, persuade, motivate and convince others, your story will remain untold. You will not get that coveted job or opportunity.

Many proactive job seekers have used creative ways to tell their stories and get hired. Throughout this book you will find examples and resources, or read stories of individuals who have done just that.

In today's competitive environment, professionals like you must become masterful storytellers; and to get a job in the current market, you need signature stories that will set you apart from the competition. You need stories that will woo your audience – whether it's an audience of one or many. To get your message across and enhance your chances for success, you need to strategically craft and deliver stories that will engage and capture your audience. That is the premise on which this book is based.

We tell stories every day – to family, friends, colleagues, clients, customers and, yes, interviewers, employers, hiring managers and recruiters! This book will help you to be clear, concise and credible when marketing yourself through various tools – social media or your career marketing documents. So, whether you are seeking a new opportunity or looking for a promotion, you need to learn how to tell stories!

Do you have a compelling **C**hallenge-**A**ction-**R**esults success story that demonstrates your value to your employer? Did you know that your résumé, and all your other career marketing efforts are all telling your story? Why do you think you are often asked to "tell me about yourself" or "describe a time when...". It's to give you an opportunity to recount stories that will convince the hiring manager to choose you. If you think about it, the entire job search process is one of storytelling, and you need to understand how it works and how it could differentiate you from others who are competing with you for the same position.

After reading this book and applying its concepts, you will experience an empowering transformation that will lead you toward discovering and unleashing your true potential. You will learn to tell stories that help you to brag without bragging, because they are your own real stories! Furthermore, you will:

- Have a clear and focused understanding of how to tell your story to get hired.
- Develop a mindset of success and be able to apply the skills learned to effectively tell stories.
- Learn step-by-step strategies that will help you tell your story, establish your credibility and reach your career goals.
- Accelerate your career and steer it out of the rut, if you are stuck.

Read on. Then write your story and tell it to get hired.

"Great stories happen to those who can tell them."

~ Ira Glass, Radio Host

Chapter 1

The Benefits of Storytelling

By Maureen McCann

> *"There isn't anyone you couldn't love – once you've heard their story."*
>
> ~ Mary Lou Kownacki, Author

Storytelling was taught to me in school. When we were asked to write stories as second-graders, I remember having to answer the traditional questions: who, what, where, when, why and how. So as a tribute to my second-grade teacher, here is an outline of the story I'm about to share with you.

Who: You
What: Your experiences
Where: Here in this book
When: Today
Why: To help you share your story with your target audience and employment market
How: Shaping a better career story

Stories are a goldmine of information and often help us to learn about one another. So here is a little story about me that I hope will provide value to you, the job seeker, in crafting a well-polished story that will help garner you the very job you seek.

After graduating university, I had the opportunity to work at a high-end retail sports store. Every Wednesday evening, after store-hours the employer would host a product knowledge (PK) evening where veteran staff would inform newer staff about the features and benefits of merchandise in the store. The owner would host these PK evenings as a way of ensuring his staff was well-informed about the product, the customer and how to sell the product to the customer. These evenings were designed around these very pillars:

- Know the products and understand the value of the products
- Understood the wants and needs of each buyer
- Translate the product's value to the want or need of the buyer (or vice versa)

In other words, in order to sell any product to a customer we needed to:

- Have an excellent understanding of the needs of the customer
- Identify what was driving their purchase
- Match their needs to the right product

Sounds simple enough, right? You'd be surprised how many times a lack of understanding on either side would prevent a sale from happening.

Fast forward 20 years and I can tell you I apply these same business principles today in the work I do as a career professional working with six-figure executives. I help them to:

1. Understand their market needs (who is their target market, and what does this target market want/need – known and unknown to the market).
2. Value and articulate what skills, talents and abilities they have to offer their target market.
3. Match No. 1 with No. 2 in a meaningful way that is easy to understand.

Before you can tell a great story, you have to have an understanding of the pieces of a great story. Below you will find a simple exercise designed to help you focus on the value you have to offer employers. Take a few moments now to complete the exercise.

Take Action...Tell Your Story

Complete the following statements without using the same descriptive word or phrase twice. The objective is to uncover what you most enjoy and value about your contributions to the world of work.

Examples:
I am helpful; I have courage; I can teach adults; I love to share my knowledge; I enjoy working with others; I want to work in a place where I am appreciated; I enjoy supportive colleagues; I want to be paid what I am worth; I need to make $60,000 a year + benefits.

Now it's your turn.

I am ____
I am ____
I am ____

I have ____
I have ____
I have ____

I can ____
I can ____
I can ____

I love to ____
I love to ____
I love to ____

I enjoy ____
I enjoy ____
I enjoy ____

I want ____
I want ____
I want ____

I need ____
I need ____
I need ____

While simple at first, you may have found yourself struggling to find the right words as you progressed. That's OK! Give yourself a break – it's not often you are asked to reflect on yourself and asked to describe yourself with so many different words. However, it is a crucial exercise to conduct prior to a job search because that is exactly what you will be asked to do in a job interview!

After completing the exercise, review it and see if you can find a common thread or a running theme within the words/phrases on the page. Once you have found it, it may fit into a sentence like this: "I have been a (teacher, helper, leader, writer, builder…) all my life." Or "Throughout my life, I have often, if not always, enjoyed (working with my hands, researching projects, writing policy, creating and innovating…)."

When you re-discover the things that bring you joy and are able to put words to them, you will enjoy and gain clarity in the following ways:

a) Awareness of self – the foundation of self-confidence (needed when promoting yourself in a job search)
b) Understanding of the value you have to offer others

c) Attentiveness to resources and connections already available within your network
d) Appropriate language and terminology to use for your skills, abilities, talents and strengths
e) Ability to articulate your value to others.

Call it serendipity, happenstance or an action plan, this new awareness and understanding will create the momentum you need to move yourself forward in today's job market. Storytelling, much like other forms of communication, is a practiced and learned art.

- **Clarity** What you have to offer
- **Focus** What the employer wants from you
- **Value Proposition** Matching what you have with what the employer wants.

Maureen McCann is Chief Career Strategist and Owner, ProMotion Career Solutions

Chapter 2

Personal Branding

> *"Stop thinking branding belongs exclusively to the marketing department. YOU are the marketing department."*
>
> ~ William Arruda & Deb Dib,
> Personal Branding Ambassadors

What is a Personal Brand?

We live and operate in a very competitive environment, and anyone who wants to distinguish him- or herself from the crowd will have to embrace the concept of personal branding.

Personal branding architect, Paul Copcutt, said: "The great news about personal brands is that everyone already has one. The key is understanding what that brand is and communicating it to the people that need to know."

To understand personal branding, you only have to think of the strategies that companies use to evoke an emotional response from consumers with respect to their products. These same strategies apply to personal branding.

Keep in mind that consumers choose between brands, employers choose between candidates.

You have watched commercials, read advertisements and made buying decisions based on the influence of advertising of brands. Personal branding is no different. In fact, employers see you as a product and look for the same characteristics or "buying motivators" when they consider you for a position. They look for these character traits while reviewing your résumé, during the interview and, once you get on board, they monitor your brand to see if it is consistently showing as you perform the job for which you were hired.

For those who are thinking personal branding is spinning a message that is a lie or trying to be someone you are not, that is not true. Personal branding is about authenticity – being yourself and highlighting the skills, knowledge and strengths that make you unique. You will need to showcase yourself in a way that feels natural to you, yet capture the attention of the hiring manager. In this type of marketing authenticity is important. You need to ensure that your brand is received positively by the people thinking of hiring you.

Develop Your Personal Brand

Here are some steps to help you understand and develop your personal brand stories for job search success:

- Identify your strengths – either using self-assessments or former employer feedback.
- Ask people who know you – friends, relatives, colleagues, managers – what their perceptions are of you.
    - What words would they use to describe you?
    - What strengths do they think you have?
    - What weaknesses do they think you have?
- Compare your findings in your assessment with the feedback from others to uncover comments that are common.
- Based on the comments, create a T-Chart, and write down your strengths on one side and your weaknesses on the other.

- Focus on your strengths to see how you can build on them.
- Evaluate your weaknesses only to the degree that it will help you become a better person, but do not spend a lot of energy on them.
- Select the characteristics that best describe who you are and package them as your "Brand Story". From that, look to identify common themes that you can highlight in career documents (résumés and cover letters) as well as in any other form of communication, including elevator speeches and responses in interviews.
- Consider the role you are applying for and who else might be competing for that job. What are the elements that you have and they will have too? What is your "added value" – that one thing that you can offer that perhaps others would not possess? Make sure you are communicating those different stories throughout your application.
- What do you know about who is receiving your application? What are the attributes they are looking for in the candidate they need to fill the vacancy?
- Can you capture, in easy-to-understand phrases or sentences, a culmination of all the above points, e.g., I use my (strengths) to help (hiring manager/company) effectively (what your job role does) by (your unique differences)?

Communicate Your Personal Brand

Once you have a clear brand statement you can focus on communicating it in a way that feels genuine and comfortable to you. Identify the various ways through which you can communicate with people and choose the ones where you come across most effectively.

Personal branding is a way of telling an authentic story that conveys the person you are, and you use that to leverage all that is great about you. You have to create a mindset that you are no longer an employee trying to find an employer to hire you but a special brand that an employer wants to "buy".

Not only will personal branding give you a formula for success for your job search, but it is also something that you can apply as you advance in your career. It means you remain true to who you are while celebrating your uniqueness and communicating your value.

A well-branded company knows its products, knows its strengths and knows how to capitalize on its strengths. Get to know "Product Me": capitalize on your strengths and tell your story.

Power Words and Phrases You Can Use In Building Your Personal Branding

Select 5-10 words or phrases that best describe you:

Assertive
Articulate
Artistic
Bilingual
Attentive to Detail
Authentic
Ambitious
Communicative
Adaptable
Accommodating
Brilliant
Budget-conscious
Compassionate
Considerate
Courteous

Fair
Flexible
Genuine
Happy
Goal-oriented
Good communicator
Generous
Insightful
Helpful
Friendly
Influencing
Humorous
Intuitive
Inspiring
Interpersonal (skills)

Objective
Open-minded
Patient
People-oriented
Persistent
Positive
Practical
Problem-solver
Professional
Proud
Quick
Quiet
Resilient
Resourceful
Respectful

Calm
Confident
Creative
Competitive
Convincing
Decisive
Diplomatic
Discreet
Driven
Dedicated
Demanding
Dynamic
Easy to get along with
Energetic
Enthusiastic
Ethical
Empowering
Encouraging

Innovative
Just
Joker
Joyful
Kind
Leader
Listener
Loyal
Logical
Manager
Motivator
Mentor
Morale-builder
Negotiator
Nice
Opportunistic
Non-judgemental
Opinionated

Responsible
Results-oriented
Self-directed
Sensitive
Sincere
Supportive
Tactful
Team player
Thoughtful
Tolerant
Troubleshooter
Trustworthy
Understanding
Useful
Visionary
Well-rounded
Willing to try new things
Work well under pressure

Chapter 3

Identifying Your Value Proposition

"I said I am great: why don't they believe me?"
~ Unknown

The term *value proposition* is similar in ways to personal branding. They both focus on who you are, what you have to offer and what differentiates you from all the other candidates vying for the same position.

Sandy Khan, an international MBA recruiter and coach, has been hiring MBA graduates for companies such as Google and Microsoft International. While her focus is on MBA graduates, the wisdom she doles out is suitable for anyone who is seeking to tell stories and get hired. In an interview with *Poets and Quants*, a website catering to existing and potential MBA grads, she underscores the importance of storytelling in the job search:

"Job seekers need to perceive themselves as products and recruiters as their buyers. They need to understand where the buyer's pain points are; what they really want and then make sure their stories demonstrate their problem-solving abilities. They then use storytelling principles to engage these recruiters, showcasing why they are the best products on the shelf."

This piece of advice helps you to understand the concept of value proposition – how can you add value to an employer and solve their problems. Your value proposition has three components:

Buying Motivators: What is the employer looking for? Where are they hurting most? Are they looking for someone to turn around a money-losing operation, rectify a technology glitch or help them increase revenue?

Supporting Qualifications: How does your qualification match the employer's buying motivators? What are the skills, abilities, education, experience, credentials and accomplishments that you have that will meet the needs of the employer? Remember that each employer is different, so one size doesn't fit all. You will need to zero in on what that specific employer needs and select those qualifications/attributes that they need.

Added Value: Your supporting qualifications are not unique. There are many other candidates competing with you. Therefore, you need to rise above your competitors and see what extra value you can bring to the employer. What do you have that's distinctly different from others? Do you have multilingual capabilities? Do you have a patent on a product? Did you create a system that solved a particular problem and saved or made money for an employer? That's your added value.

Once you are able to tie these three components together – **Buying Motivators**, **Supporting Qualifications** and **Added Value** – you are ready to articulate your value proposition and develop your brand statement.

Chapter 4

Introverts Have Powerful Stories Too

> *"In a society where we are expected to dazzle and be dazzled, from pitching venture capitalists by day to rubbing against high-powered elbows at night, introverts are often thought of as out-casts who quietly lurk in the margins."*
>
> ~ Nancy Acowitz, Author

I have included this chapter on introverts based on Susan Cain's book **Quiet: The Power of Introverts in a World That Can't Stop Talking**. Most people associate introversion with shyness or the ability to speak up. That's not always the case. Bill Gates, Richard Branson, Rosa Parks, Mahatma Ghandi, Abraham Lincoln, Warren Buffett and Michael Jordan – faces of the past and present – are considered introverts, yet that did not prevent them from telling their stories and making invaluable contributions to society.

Why a chapter about introverts? First of all, I give the impression most times that I am one of these "life-of-the-party" extroverts, when, in fact, I am an introvert parading as an extrovert. Many people are shocked to hear this from me, but it is true.

Recently I was at an event, and while others were busy networking during breaks, I remained in my seat doing everything else other than networking. I did make an effort to saunter over and connect with the three main speakers, but this is not something I do very well. I like going out, but if given the choice, I would stay home, watch sports and/or politics, read a book or write for leisure.

While this topic is somewhat personal, I have included it because of a conversation I had with a client some months ago. An accomplished finance analyst, he is as sharp as a razor when interacting one-on-one but a basket-case during job interviews. He struggles to sell himself and tell stories of his accomplishments. One reason is that he is measured in his thought process, preferring to think things out carefully before speaking. This, he was told in one case, was a deficit, as they were looking for "someone who can think quickly on their feet".

Among my recommendations to him, was Susan Cain's popular 19-minute *TedTalk* video, **The Power of Introverts**. That was an eye-opener for him.

So this chapter is in recognition of that segment of the population who are introverts and many, like me, who are parading as extroverts. Introverts, too, have their stories, but society pays so much attention to the extroverts of the world that the stories of many introverts are often untold. Many have lost out on opportunities because they were not seen as confident and outgoing and just did not fit the mould.

Susan Cain says: "Our most important institutions, our schools and our workplaces, they are designed mostly for extroverts and for extroverts' need for lots of stimulation." She goes on to say that "this is our loss for sure, but it is also our colleagues' loss and our communities' loss. And at the risk of sounding grandiose, it is the world's loss. Because when it comes to creativity and to leadership, we need introverts doing what they do best."

If there is any truth that introverts make up one-third to 50 percent of the population, that's a fairly huge chunk of people who are quietly going about their business doing what they do best. The fact that they prefer solitary activity to group situations should not be construed as being shy, aloof or afraid.

Recognize that their preference for solitude gives them a sense of control and a space to regroup; that they make great team members, and they add diverse perspectives to solving problems. The old proverb "silent river runs deep" pretty much sums up an introvert: they might not say much, but underneath they have much to offer.

Although the following seven job search tips apply to any job seeker, introverts will definitely find them useful:

1. **Know yourself:** Candidly assess your strengths, weaknesses, failures and successes, and be ready to address them if asked.

2. **Articulate your strengths:** Discuss your ability to be quiet and reflective; that you work well independently and in teams.

3. **Be authentic:** Don't try to be somebody you are not because it will become evident as the conversation goes on.

4. **Strengthen your online presence.** Nothing speaks louder than a well-written, consistent online profile. This could be a personal website or a LinkedIn profile, complete with accomplishments and work samples (if appropriate).

5. **Review interview questions.** While you may not know all the questions you will be asked, research, review and practice the ones that are commonly asked.

6. **Learn to promote yourself.** This might take you out of your comfort zone but learn to talk about yourself. If you don't, then people will not know the broad range of your talents

7. **Realize that networking is not always a numbers game.** The fact that the extroverts are handing out as many business cards as they can does not mean you should do the same. It is better to connect and have conversations with two or three quality contacts than have 20 or 30 names in a database.

Chapter 5

Developing an Elevator Speech

> *"Your elevator speech is a verbal business card or billboard. In order for it to be effective, it must be compelling."*
>
> ~ Leah Grant, Consultant

One quick way to tell people your story is to develop a storytelling "elevator speech". This immediately lets people know who you are, what field you are in, what distinguishes you from everyone else, and how an employer can benefit from your skills. The term is quite common and is based on the premise that it should take you no longer than a 30-second elevator ride to introduce yourself to someone in a memorable way.

These days, you may not have as much as 30 seconds, so it is being suggested that you also create a seven- to 10-second spiel. An effective elevator speech, whether seven or 30 seconds, is a short introduction that markets you as an individual or promotes your business.

Your elevator speech is as essential as your calling or business card and résumé. If you do not have a strong storytelling elevator speech, it becomes harder for you to communicate what you really do. Before you can convince anyone that they should really pay attention to you, you must know yourself – know exactly what you have to offer, what problems you can solve and what benefits you bring to a prospective contact or employer.

You will also realize that developing your elevator speech parallels creating your personal branding statement. The processes are similar. Use the following questions to help you create your elevator speech:

- What are my key strengths? What am I good at?
- What words come to mind when I describe myself or when someone describes me?
- What is it I am trying to let others know about me?

Your next step is to prepare an outline of your story based on:

- Who am I?
- What do I have to offer?
- What problems have I solved?
- What are the main contributions I can make?
- What should my contact or the employer do as a result of hearing my story?

Begin by jotting down a few simple bullet points – phrases to remind you of what you really want to say. Use benefit-focused terminology to convince the person that you have the right knowledge, skills and experience.

When you have answered all the questions above, you are ready to finalize your story. Go back through the notes and expand on each point. Make sure the final result contains no more than 100 words.

Remember, you are trying to tell your contacts or the employer a convincing and memorable story about you in 30 seconds. Make sure you achieve that goal.

Chapter 6

Building a Social Media Job Search Campaign

"We don't have a choice on whether we do social media, the question is how well we do it?"

~Erik Qualman, Author

There is a popular quote that says, "If you always do what you have always done, you will always get what you always got." If that's what you have been doing without much success, it's time to suspend all that you know about the job search, stop doing what everyone is doing, and try something different, scary, and unconventional. After all, what do you have to lose?

For too long you have been engaged in "push marketing" where you are sending résumés to every possible company and contact. But your résumé is being "lost" in the résumé black hole and not getting to the decision maker. It's time to engage in "pull marketing" where you become a target for potential employers.

Here are some reasons to embrace this concept. A personal social media campaign will:

- Differentiate you from your competition – all those vying for the same position you are after.
- Give you opportunities to engage with your target employers, connect with colleagues working in your industry and expand your network.

- Allow you to leverage your brand using LinkedIn, Twitter, Facebook, Google+ and other platforms where recruiters will discover you and learn about you.

If you have a LinkedIn, Twitter, Facebook or Google+ account, you already have the tools to begin. Participate in discussions on these forums where your target employers are. It is pointless to join social media groups without becoming an active participant. That's like attending a meeting but not contributing to the discussion. Ask and answer questions, give or request opinions on your areas of interest, create your own discussion topics or write articles that will generate conversations.

Do not hesitate to comment on a company's blog. There is a story of a young man from Oregon who tried for two years to get a job at Microsoft. It wasn't until he started to contribute to conversations on the company's blog that they took notice and hired him 10 days after he was discovered. A well-defined social media job search strategy will help boost your reputation and have employers seeking you out rather than the other way around. It also helps you stand out from your competition who, in all likelihood, is spending all their time on push marketing.

Here is a simple way to start your campaign:

- Find a blog post, a tweet or an article from one of the employers you would like to work for.
- Read it thoroughly. Decide if you would like to ask a question or give your opinion about it. If someone has already made comments, engage in the dialogue to showcase your expertise.
- Don't let it end there. Take the conversation to your preferred social media platform. Offer it as an update on LinkedIn where people in your network could "Like" it, or offer their own comments. Take the discussion to one of your LinkedIn groups to garner additional exposure.

In a *Fast Company* article, the writer tells a story of how a 16-year-old high school student emailed her and asked to join her as a guest on her TV show. He did not send a résumé, but instead included links to his website, Twitter account, Facebook page, and three relevant YouTube clips. (This kid had launched his own social media campaign!). This initiative earned him an invitation to be a guest on the show.

Build a Personal Website

According to *The Daily Muse*, "Building an online presence is more important than ever. It doesn't matter if you're looking for a career change (when recruiters are sure to Google you), or if you just need a place to share your personal story – how you appear on the web shapes what people think of you."

Yes, a personal website is a must for anyone who wants to tell their career story and get hired, and these days it is so easy! Most of these tools are free, with fill-in-the-blank templates, you don't have to be a technical expert or have programming expertise. And, while you are at it, lay claim to your name and register it as your domain name if it's not already taken.

You may be saying to yourself that you already have other online profiles – what's the point in getting yet another? Because, your personal website is a part of your brand-building process, and the best way to begin is to claim your name, assuming it is still available. You will then use your personal website as a one-stop haven for your other social media profiles like LinkedIn, Facebook, Twitter, Google+ and YouTube (if you're venturing into videos).

When employers and recruiters begin searching for you, or when you need to connect with someone of influence, it's easy to send them a link to your own website which houses your other profiles.

Create Your Social Profile

By Maureen McCann

Social profiles are a reflection of who you are. So who are you? What information do you want to share with prospective employers and colleagues? Before you can answer this question, put yourselves in the employer's position. Imagine you were reviewing four online profiles and came across the following four situations. What assumptions might you make about the following people?

1. Email address: partyanimal@hotmail.com*
2. Current position: Currently seeking employment
3. LinkedIn profile: 25 per cent profile completeness
4. Connections: 500+ connections (no recommendations or testimonials)

a) The first example is a real situation that happened to me. My husband and I have a cottage that we rent out on a weekly basis. One day I received an email from *partyanimal@hotmail.com**. Whether or not it was fair, I jumped to a conclusion about this person: What they and their friends would be like? What damage they would cause to my cottage? And, before any further exchanges took place, deleted the email, never to hear from that email address again. (*The email address has been changed for privacy reasons).

b) While there are a number of career professionals who recommend advertising your current employment status online as "available for immediate assignment" or something similar, I would much prefer a client have a robust online profile that proudly features his/her recent accomplishments and downplays his/her current unemployed status. "Currently seeking employment", in my opinion, reeks of desperation. It immediately triggers questions in my mind: What is wrong with this person? Did they get fired? Were they bad at their job?

Another possible scenario I ran through: Can this person not think of a better way to present himself or herself online? Is this the kind of first impression they are OK with? If so, do I want them representing my brand? Now, this may seem harsh, and again, a little unfair. However it is good for you to be aware so you don't make these types of errors when telling your online story. Do you agree?

c) I once told a group of women at Ottawa's Girl Geek Dinner that an incomplete online profile tells a story of someone who is satisfied with incomplete work! Does that accurately describe who you are? No, of course not. So whatever you choose to do online (whether it be LinkedIn, Twitter, Facebook, Pinterest – whatever) do it to the best of your ability. That does not mean you have to do them all at the same time. It means start with one – maybe LinkedIn – and work on your profile until it is 100 per cent complete and you are 100 per cent satisfied with it! There are plenty of online tutorials, webinars, books and blog posts written about how to write a stellar profile, So do your homework, then get writing!

d) This is a pet peeve of mine. Five or so years ago, I noticed lots of people connecting to one another on LinkedIn to improve the number of connections they had. Now this seems a little counter-intuitive to me: It is not the number of people in your life, it is the quality of people you are connecting with. Anyway, I find it difficult to imagine that someone could know over 500 people and not one of them would be interested in writing a testimonial or a recommendation on their behalf! If you are updating your online profile, take a few moments to invite others to write about you. You would be surprised how much more credible your profile becomes with just a few testimonials.

There is no way to ensure or guarantee consistent results because everyone comes to your online profile with their own beliefs and diverse perspective. Your job is to take the guess-work out of your profile and tell a meaningful story about who you are and what makes you great!

Maureen McCann is Chief Career Strategist and Owner, ProMotion Career Solutions

Tell Your Professional Story on LinkedIn

In an article on *Inc.com*, Steve Cody wrote a compelling piece on how to tell your professional story on LinkedIn. While the article focused on LinkedIn, the advice is applicable across all social media platforms.

LinkedIn is an international business networking site where you can find former colleagues, connect with industry experts and search job postings. Already, there are over 300 million registered users, including executives from Fortune 500 companies, many of whom are using this networking site to recruit staff.

"People think LinkedIn is a place where they keep their résumé online and maybe have some connections with people they know professionally. They don't think of it as a place to get business intelligence, to research problems, [or] to establish an online presence where other people in the network can find them," says Reid Hoffman, Co-Founder of LinkedIn.

A good LinkedIn profile gives an account of your career trajectory – how you have grown professionally and what your achievements and professional choices have been. It is probably the most significant channel to tell your professional story and get hired.

Therefore, whether or not you are in a job search mode, it is important that you have a LinkedIn profile. Why? Recruiters and potential employers are more likely to search for candidates like you online.

At one point it was thought that LinkedIn profiles should be written in a formal third-person format. However, with social media, it is acceptable to be less formal yet still maintain your professionalism. Use the first-person format and make sure that you are using most, if not all, of the 2,000 character spaces LinkedIn allows you to write a compelling summary story.

Another advantage of LinkedIn is that your contacts can introduce you to their contacts. There is no better way to meet potential employers than being recommended by a mutual contact. On LinkedIn, your profile is accessible to the hundreds of recruiters who are there looking for people like you. In fact, while your résumé will generally get a limited number of eyeballs, a LinkedIn profile, which is 100 per cent completed (or close) and is rich with keywords, has the potential to garner more views and, therefore, more opportunities.

Below are some tips on how you can create or improve your LinkedIn and social profile to make sure it is telling your story. Some of these tips are excerpts originally contributed to **No Canadian Experience, Eh!** by career coach Cecile Peterkin:

- Provide a clear picture of who you are, how you have succeeded in the past and what you want to do. LinkedIn is enormously popular with recruiters and is viewed as much more effective for the job search than job boards.
- Request LinkedIn recommendations from people who can attest to your work and character.
- Establish connections with people working at potential employers who could help you network towards a job.

- Add your job search email address to your profile summary so it will be easy for employers to reach you.
- Include the accomplishments from your résumé in your profile summary as well.
- Make your personal headline a summary of your target job.
- Join appropriate LinkedIn groups and participate (carefully!) in group discussions. This is a good way to demonstrate your knowledge, language skills and interests.
- Keep your profile up to date, add connections and recommendations, and stay active in the groups that are most important and relevant to your work.
- If you are using social media for job searching, remember your photo is most often the first impression that people will get of you. It is important that your photo is clear, appropriate and professional. Social media is about being open and sharing, not hiding behind icons or blank images.
- Social media is the modern means of networking. In any job search, you are in the business of promoting yourself. Learning to ride the wave of social media through sites such as Twitter and LinkedIn will make you more marketable, expand your networks and help to improve your opportunity to find and land that ideal job.

Chapter 7

Networking Strategies

By Wayne Pagani

> *The key to all successful networking for job search is to build relationships first, ask for assistance second and offer to be of assistance always.*
>
> ~ Unknown

To me networking is as natural as breathing. We all do it, and it's really more of a question of style and intensity. When it comes to job search, and business and career development, networking plays a critical role in a person's ability to navigate the landscape and achieve mutual objectives.

The following stories are intended to help you gain a better insight into the value of networking and possibly provide a few techniques that will prove helpful to you.

My Mentee's Story

I am a volunteer mentor with a local service organization that matches internationally-educated professionals with professionals in the local market. One of my mentees, a newcomer to Canada, was not accustomed to networking and not really sure that he understood how it worked or why he would want to engage in such activities. All he wanted was a fair chance to secure a job in his field, either as an electrical engineer or as an academic instructor in a college or university.

Get Started at the Beginning: Rather than trying to convince him that he needed to network as part of the job search process, instead I asked about industry associations related to his field and the designations professionals in his field might need to gain recognition. I also asked if he might be open to exploring other venues where we could both learn more about what is happening in the fields that he was targeting and the roles that we might be applying for in the future.

Look for Peers and Like-minded People: He indicated that he was a long-time member of the Institute of Electrical and Electronics Engineers (IEEE); however, he had not attended events here in Ottawa. As a result of our discussions, he started attending functions in various milieus, including IEEE events and meetings with people in his field. He eventually met a professor from the Electrical Engineering department at Ottawa University at an IEEE forum.

In the Right Place at the Right Time: My mentee did not go in asking everyone he met for a job; he simply spoke about something he already has a passion for – electrical engineering. It was not long before the Ottawa University professor invited my mentee to prepare and present on a topic related to electrical engineering. This ultimately led to a job offer and short-term contract – all because he put himself in a situation where the likelihood of this happening was higher.

My Story – Planting the Seed

In 1994, I worked with the Personal Growth Centre, an organization based in Montreal that helped people to get their lives back on track, where I introduced their services and developed business on their behalf. This led me to make an appointment with CanCare in Ottawa, one of the largest Employee Assistance Programs in Canada at the time.

Let People Know Your Goals: Prior to leaving Montreal, I shared with friends and associates that I was heading to Ottawa for a meeting with CanCare. By the time I left for the appointment I had received at least ten more names of people in different organizations in Ottawa who I could meet during my stay.

What started out to be an afternoon journey and about a two-hour car ride to Ottawa turned into a week-long business trip and an unexpected adventure. After meeting with CanCare, I went to several appointments which turned out to be fruitful. By the end of the week, I had made new contacts and left with approximately 30 more names. In the process, I also received a new contract offer.

When I returned to Montreal, I made the decision to explore the Ottawa market further. I have lived here ever since. So how did this happen, you might ask?

Without realizing it, many of us do the same thing that I experienced when I decided to meet with CanCare. Only we often do so unconsciously and, as a result, miss the opportunity. As a career coach, I was told by so many people that finding employment in the past really took place more by association. However, many of these same people are stymied today when we use terminology like "networking" to secure their next job.

As soon as people try to network and, depending on their connotation of the word, the "process" can become intimidating for some, daunting for others, and stressful for many when the stakes are high and a potential job hangs in the balance. And this is typically the reason many fail at networking. All the focus in their "networking" activities is on getting a job.

Networking = Relationship Building: It's been my experience that networking, true networking, isn't about having an objective and leveraging others to serve that objective. It's about relationship building and, ironically, as a by-product of forming and nurturing these relationships, somehow the support, resources, information and people needed to achieve these objectives begin to appear.

That's not to say that you'll wave a magical networking wand and, abracadabra, a job appears. You still need to be tuned in and be aware of what's happening around you. The difference is that it starts by giving, not taking: looking for ways to bring win-win scenarios to fruition for all and remaining authentically committed to what makes you tick.

Duplicate the Process: Over the years, I have become more cognizant of how relationship building and networking with people have ended up supporting me and vice-versa. So I have learned to direct the process and take advantage of every opportunity to get involved and connected. When it comes to my career and business, I have joined various associations related to the career development field. Participation in these groups have led to many new friendships and lasting relationships, some of which have turned into fruitful alliances and collaborations.

I invite you to do the same in your career. Yes, right now your need might be to simply find a job that can help to pay the bills and provide sustenance. However, by starting to look at the bigger picture and with an investment in your longer-term career development road map, the relationship building process and networking activities that you engage in today will continue to pay huge dividends to you in the future.

One Client's Story

Recently, one of my newer clients identified that he needed to improve his networking skills. After completing a thorough networking assessment, we were able to explore an accurate picture of how he saw himself and what networking meant to him. This also helped to identify his strengths and weaknesses in networking. By doing so, we could see where he possessed skills that would help in his networking activities.

As we spoke about his strengths and some of the elements to be effective and successful in networking, he suddenly recounted several stories where he had indeed been very effective with networking. One of which was a great "pay it forward" experience, that had left quite an impression on him.

There are several networking assessments online. Find one that works for you and assess your networking ability. You may just be pleasantly surprised.

Evaluation Scale

1 to 5 (5 being the highest)		
Style	Score	Comments
Strong sense of community		
Working alone and independently		
Enjoy public engagements and speaking		

Some Takeaways from These Stories:

- Pay it forward
- Get involved – networking is an action verb
- Find out what people/organizations need and offer ways to help them fill that need

- Develop a reputation – be known for the value that you share with others
- Become a subject matter expert in your field
- If you don't know many people – go to where the people are
- Connect with like-minded people (maybe even other job seekers to get started)
- Be in the right place at the right time

Wayne Pagani is the Owner & Principal Consultant of W. P. Consulting & Associates

Take Action...Tell Your Story

The following is an action plan for integrating networking activities into your job search:

Action Items:

1) Set and follow through on your objectives:
   a) Attend one lunch meeting per week – keep these simple, then build to more meetings per week.
   b) Use these informal meetings to practice and assess yourself.
   c) Practice the art of small talk by identifying common interests – what works and what doesn't.
   d) Return to the networking assessment to refer to your strengths and weaknesses.
   e) Keep a running journal to track your progress.

2) Market research – start looking for those organizations with a need that fits your value proposition.

3) Build Community:
   a) Start attending some of the groups or events that you already know about.

b) Peruse Event Brite, Meet Up (or other meet up sites) and find regular events to meet people.
c) Investigate local events with the intent of meeting at least one person each time.
d) Set another objective for yourself to attend a specific number of events within a certain time on a regular basis.

4) Apply the principles that you learn from different resources to fuel your desire to improve your ability for relationship building, including:
   a) **The Connect Effect** by Michael Dulworth
   b) **Never Eat Alone** and **Who's Got Your Back?** by Keith Ferrazzi
   c) **Six Pixels of Separation** by Mitch Joel (also available on CD)

5) Look for venues and opportunities to practice and environments that are supportive where you can fine-tune your skills. Here are a few ideas to get you started:
   a) Toastmasters International
   b) Canadian Association of Public Speakers (CAPS)
   c) Speed Networking events
   d) Job Finding Clubs (or start one on your own)

6) Orient yourself to networking. This is critical in a job search, especially for those who either lack the skills, the awareness or feel intimidated by networking. Begin to label or identify your network as follows:

   A – Already known contacts
   B – Bridging contacts
   C – Critical contacts (either gate keepers to opportunities or hiring managers themselves)

These are the ABC's to networking that can be an effective way to layout the landscape for people who are not sure where to start. Of course, with today's technological advancements, there are plenty of resources that can help do this as well.

7) Get organized:
   a) Keep track of your network and networking activities using online tools such as *JibberJobber* which is a career management tool.

Networking With the 'Newly Departed'

One of the stalwarts of the recruiting industry is David Perry, Managing Partner of Perry Martel, an executive search firm based in Ottawa, Ontario, Canada. David has put a new spin on how job candidates can engage employers to land their next job, and it has nothing to do with dead people, as the term "newly-departed" might suggest. The information below is a summary of an interview I had with David.

Over the last 20 years people have gotten used to doing what are called informational interviews. A lot of people will select the top ten companies they want to work for regardless of whether that company is advertising for someone or not. They then try to network their way into those companies so they can discover what the problems are with the company and how they might be able to help fix the problem.

"Informational interviews are great," David said, "but there is a better way, and we call it 'networking with the newly departed'." But this is not about connecting with dead people, he stated.

As he explained it, a job candidate in need of a position need to target at least ten companies and then use *Google* to do a keyword search, or use LinkedIn to find people who used to work at the companies from six months to a year ago. Give them a call them and say, "Hi ______ my name is ______. I know you used to work at XYZ Corporation. I'm doing research and would like to ask you a couple of questions about the company. Is this a good time?"

Nine out of 10 times even the most timid person will get a "Yes. What do you want to know?" You then proceed to ask them as many questions as you can, he added.

One such question is: "From your perspective what are the three biggest issues your former department and boss are facing in the business?" Listen attentively and take notes, David said.

He noted that the person will tell you what the burning issues are. You will then follow up with a question: "Who was your direct supervisor, and what was he or she like to work with?"

David said that you will most likely get honest answers because that individual no longer works with that company and there is no reason for them not to share that information.

He noted that the answers to those and other questions will paint a clear picture of what a company's real issues are. From there you should be able to figure out what accomplishments or experience you have that can solve the issues. This is important because when you write your résumé and cover letter to that executive – the most senior person that is responsible for the problem – you can tell them exactly what their needs are and present your accomplishments that match those needs.

You may be saying to yourself that these busy executives might not have the time to connect with you. But David pointed out that it does not matter whether you are an entry-level new graduate or a senior executive, if you can present a convincing story of how you will be able to solve a problem, then anyone, including the executive, will listen to you.

This is not the time to be shy, but time to think of unconventional strategies to engage potential employers and land your next job.

Why You Need to Network to Get Work

Networking guru Donna Messer said that one has to "network to get work". It doesn't matter how often you hear this; it doesn't matter how often you discount it, networking to get work is a fact.

Too often people say, "networking doesn't work for me...I am too shy to network...people might think I am forcing myself on them". Some of these comments may be true, but let's GOI – Get Over It. Don't allow such crippling thoughts to prevent you from getting the job or promotion you really want or deserve.

You may be telling yourself that you have a great résumé and cover letter, but not much is happening. Well, by themselves, they won't get you the opportunity you are looking for. You need to find creative ways to use these documents to reach your target company. It takes hard work, and lots of it!

Thomas Edison once said, "Opportunity is missed by most people because it is dressed in overalls and looks like hard work." Do not miss your opportunity because you are thinking networking is hard work. I can guarantee you, if done properly, your networking efforts will pay off. Just don't expect overnight success!

Some years ago, I was listening to a group of recruiters on a teleseminar. One was a senior executive recruiter from Microsoft. He told the story of a young man who had been trying to get a job with the company for two years. His résumé was just not getting to the right people. You bet it was probably drowning in the sea of thousands of other résumés.

This young man discovered that the company had several blogs, and began to offer comments and contribute his opinions on topics that fell within his area of expertise. One of the company's recruiters began paying attention to his comments and posts, and realized he knew his stuff. Not very long after he was contacted, and within 10 days of that contact he was offered his dream job with Microsoft. This may have been several years ago, but the process still works. You have to ditch the idea that networking doesn't work, and devise strategies on how you are going to make it work for you.

One of my clients saw a position with one of his target companies and remembered I knew one of the senior HR executives, so he sent me an email to ask if I was still in touch with her. I hadn't been for a long time, so I googled her name and realized she had moved out of that role. However, while doing the search, I found an article with the name of another recruiter in the company. I passed it to the client and suggested that he do a little bit of footwork and find out how email addresses at the company are structured. Soon after, he responded:

"Thanks for the article. I had a friend who previously worked at (Company) so I was able to copy that format and send a message through to the lady from the article. She said she had switched positions but would forward my message to a finance recruiter. Hopefully that will help speed things along."

That's networking and research all wrapped in one. Somewhere out there, there is an employer who needs what you have to offer. But you need to know how to get on their radar. You can do this by tapping into your network or the network of others. If the thought of networking sends shivers down your spine, don't try doing it alone. Ask for help.

Chapter 8

Body Language Speaks Louder Than Words

"What you do speaks so loud that I cannot hear what you say."
~ Ralph Waldo Emerson,
American essayist and poet

How many times have you heard that "actions speak louder than words?" It is true. Our thoughts and feelings, and the messages we send through non-verbal body language, tell a more authentic story than the words we speak. Body language consists of non-verbal communication such as facial expressions, eye movements, gestures and posture.

People are good at interpreting our body language. Is our smile one of happiness or disapproval? Do we show interest with our eyes or do we roll them in disgust? Do we lean forward to demonstrate interest and acceptance or do we slump to show discouragement? When it comes to gestures, do we nod our heads to show approval and agreement, or do we tap our fingers to show boredom or impatience? All these expressions have an impact on how we are viewed by people.

One of the biggest determinants to job search success is how we communicate. The communication mistake that many people make is to focus mostly on our ability to talk and write, forgetting that non-verbal communication makes up approximately 93 per cent of how we communicate.

Body language experts say that when we are communicating face-to-face, seven per cent is based on what we say and 93 per cent is based on our non-verbal communication – our attitude and appearance. When broken down further, 55 per cent is based on what people see and 38 per cent is based on our tone of voice. When we are communicating through the telephone, 70 per cent is based on our tone of voice while 30 per cent is based on our words.

These are very important statistics to keep in mind when we meet people and, contrary to the saying "never judge a book by its cover", it doesn't work that way all the time. We are judged by "our covers" long before we get an opportunity to confirm or disprove people's first impressions. Therefore, in preparing for interviews or other meetings, make sure you have a good understanding of what your body language is saying.

Facial expression: Every now and again, take a look in the mirror to see the expression on your face while you are relaxing. Are you happy with your appearance? Is your face smiling back at you? An interviewer will be looking in your face to see your reaction and response to questions. Even if you mask your answer, your face will still show it. Put on a genuine smile. There's a popular quote that reads "a smile is a curve that keeps things straight". You want to keep things straight during and after the interview.

Eye contact: Are you in the habit of looking the other way when speaking with people? In some cultures it is considered rude to look a person in authority in the face. However, in North America, it's different. If you want to score points with the interviewer, make sure you maintain eye contact. This shows them that you are confident and honest, and that you have nothing to hide. Maintaining eye contact does not mean you should stare at the individual either, because that may lead them to believe that you are hostile.

Handshake: In business, the official way to greet people is with a handshake. How is yours? Is it firm, and does it convey confidence and respect? Is it limp like wet noodles or hard like a knuckle cracker? No one wants to shake hands with someone who barely offers the tips of the fingers or someone attempting to crush their finger bones.

Seating: Never take a seat until you are invited to do so. Once seated, make sure to sit upright, but in a relaxed manner. Do not slouch nor sit on the edge of the chair. This will give the impression that you are nervous and lack confidence.

Hand gestures: "Watch your hands, watch your hands, where they go!" That may be a catchy phrase from kindergarten, but it is quite applicable in the world of business. Sit with your hands in your lap to appear calm and confident, but never cross them in front of your chest. This gives the impression that you are distant, cold and defensive. It's all right to use hand gestures to help bring your point across, as long as it is not distracting and aggressive.

Feet and legs: Place your feet flat on the floor. If you have to cross your legs, do so at the ankles under the desk where no one will see. If you sit with your ankle on your knee you will appear too casual and this could hurt your chances in the interview.

Chapter 9

Dressing to Impress

> *"The way we dress affects the way we think, the way we feel, the way we act, and the way others react to us."*
>
> ~ Judith Rasband, Image Consultant

The story you tell in the way you are dressed sends a strong signal to people, negatively or positively. It is said that if you want to earn a high-income figure you must look expensive. Without even uttering a word, people will make assumptions based on your clothing.

According to image experts, 55 per cent of another person's perception of you is based on how you look. While many companies support a "business casual" dress code, it is vitally important that you make an effort to look polished and professional for interviews or business meetings.

As alluded to earlier, first impression counts and the right outfit in the right colours allows you to create a positive impression that stands out from your competition. Men usually look good in a tailored suit or a nice shirt and slacks, but because women's fashions are more diverse, they should pay attention to what they wear and how it's worn.

Here is a suggested dress code checklist for both genders:

Women

- Solid colour, conservative suit
- Coordinated blouse
- Limited jewellery
- Moderate shoes
- Neat, professional hairstyle
- Sparse make-up & perfume
- Manicured nails

Men

- Solid colour, conservative suit and tie
- White long sleeve short
- Very limited jewellery
- Dark socks, formal shoes
- Neat, professional hairstyle
- Limited use of aftershave
- Neatly trimmed nails

If you are not sure about the dress code of the company you're interviewing with, you can call and ask or park in front of the building or the parking lot to observe what employees are wearing.

What's in a Colour

When deciding on an outfit to wear to an interview or business meeting, colours matter as much as the clothing. While the suggestions below are not keep etched in stone, they are worth reviewing before you decide on an outfit for your important interview or meeting.

Blue: The popular colour for most people, including probably, your interviewer. It emanates calm, tranquillity, confidence and authority. Blue, particularly navy, is recommended for interviews as it signifies loyalty and control.

Black: Suggests power and authority. It is stylish and timeless, but could give the impression you are unapproachable. On the other hand, if you want to convey an image as a leader or decision maker wearing black may be an option.

Gray: Highly recommended for interviews as it represents sophistication, neutrality and confidence. Also, since it is not a distracting colour, it is easy for the interviewer to focus on what you are saying instead of on what you are wearing.

Brown: Denotes reliability and stability and promotes better communication. It is another colour that is recommended for interviews.

White: Projects cleanliness and simplicity, and is a great addition to suits.

Red: A very intense and aggressive colour; it is not recommended for interviews unless it's being worn as an accent, such as a scarf or tie.

Yellow: Is an attention-getter and is not recommended for interviews as it could be overpowering.

Green: Symbolizes nature – calming and refreshing. Dark green signifies masculinity, conservativeness and wealth.

No matter what you wear, clothes should be neat and clean, and shoes nicely polished. While your mode of dress and the colours you choose play a role, what really matters is the ability for you to tell a story that markets your skills, experience and potential, and convince the interviewer you should be their obvious choice.

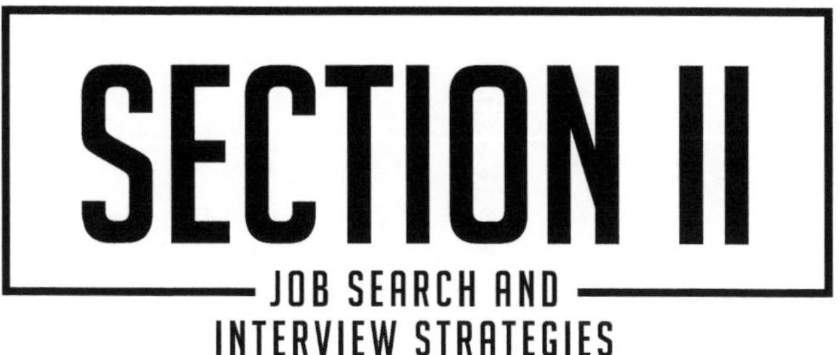

"Great storytelling can make the difference between someone paying attention to you and someone just tuning you out."

~ Christopher S. Penn,
Marketing & Media Specialist

Chapter 10

Storytelling Tools for the Job Search

By Kimberly Robb Baker

"Great marketing is storytelling."
~ Seth Godin, Author, Entrepreneur

The traditional approach to résumé writing, and marketing in general, is to build value by describing who you have helped and how you help them. If you can get this down, you'll already have one of the best résumés in the market.

But incorporating a story takes things to a whole new level. It gives the reader insight into *why* you do what you do. If the reader resonates with your "why", he or she will feel compelled to meet with you, whether or not your data is perfectly aligned with the job requisition.

Since we're on the subject of stories, I'll use a couple of them to illustrate the power – and limitations – of storytelling in a résumé.

Story 1

Los Angeles, 2001: A saleswoman was driving down the Ventura Freeway to her next meeting. Her radio was tuned to 97.1 FM, KLSX, LA's biggest talk station and a fine enough way to pass time while sitting in traffic. A commercial got her attention. The station was looking for representatives to sell radio ads. With commission, a candidate could make $200,000 a year or more – about four times what our heroine was bringing home selling relocation services. She pulled over to write down the fax number and contact name.

That night, she didn't sleep. She put together a kind of résumé that described her as a sister station to 97.1, mimicking the station's daytime line-up and referencing inside jokes of each show to highlight her humour, work ethic and tenacity at making sales. The style and format of the résumé demonstrated that she knew the station well and was creative. She was called in for an interview where she learned that thousands of submissions had been received. She even got the job offer on the spot, though a pre-requisite was prior radio industry experience that she didn't have.

Story 2

"Did you write this résumé yourself?" the recruiter asked a job fair candidate.

"Yes, I did," said the candidate, trying to temper her pride to not have a doesn't-everyone-submit-masterpieces-like-this kind of tone.

The candidate quickly shifted the conversation. She was a salesperson after all, and she knew the most important thing was to connect with the other person, hear their needs and help if possible.

She got home to realize she'd made a terrible and obvious faux pas on her résumé. So that was why the recruiter had asked who wrote it! The candidate was offered the job despite the big résumé mistake.

The takeaway lessons from these two stories are:

- Using a story and creativity in your résumé can open doors (like getting an interview and job offer when thousands apply).
- The résumé isn't everything. After all, the second story is about a woman who was offered a job because she connected in person, and her conversation landed her an offer despite having a huge error on her résumé.
- While a professional writer is nice to have around, you can do this yourself! These are both stories from my personal experience *before* I learned the art of professional résumé writing.

So, do your best but don't be stressed!

Let's look at the reasons stories work in a résumé and how you can incorporate them professionally.

Write a Stellar Résumé

While it is one of the most important tools in your search, a résumé alone will not get you a job. Your résumé is a marketing document. Its purpose is to "make a sale", to move the reader to make a decision.

The biggest decision the résumé influences is whether or not you are called to an interview.

It also:

- Serves as a roadmap for the interview, giving you control over the conversation.
- Supports your interviewer's decision to move you forward in the process. After all, your interviewer will be forwarding the finalists' résumés to his colleagues or boss.

- Adds value to your candidacy, bolstering your negotiating power when it's time to agree on compensation.

Who Needs a Résumé?

There are many executives and specialized professionals who have never had a résumé because they are so much in demand that job offers come to them.

Before you start to envy these people, keep in mind that they do not always negotiate compensation as well as they could and often find their career planning them, rather than the other way around.

If you are in a challenging job transition, take heart. This is an opportunity to define yourself and be deliberate with your career plans.

Why Storytelling Works in a Résumé

If the primary purpose of the résumé is to move the reader to bring you in for an interview, then it must be persuasive. Brain and behavioural research shows that, conservatively, 50 per cent of people make decisions based on their emotions. Some sources say that all people make decisions based on emotions, but that "analytical" people justify those decisions with data.

A good story-based résumé taps into emotions while providing the needed data. Though there will never be agreement on what makes a "good résumé", this approach will give most readers what they need to make a decision.

Why should I target my résumé?
I'm willing to do anything!

Trying to unify very different goals (or just being "open to anything") will greatly lower your effectiveness. Résumés get interviews when they present solutions to the specific problem that has been keeping the reader up at night. If yours does not, it will take many more tries to get an interview.

An unfocused résumé will result in being compared, like a commodity, to other candidates with similar years of experience, education, certifications, etc. In the absence of a candidate who demonstrates unique value, the job will likely be unfilled or go to the candidate willing to accept the lowest compensation.

If your résumé is targeted and practically exploding with your one-of-a-kind ability to solve the hiring manager's most pressing challenges, you will be the candidate of choice at the right company. Your chances of professional fulfillment and an above-average compensation will increase exponentially.

Empathy for the Hero (Hint: You are Not the Hero)**:** When people read stories, they empathize with the protagonist. The protagonist in your résumé is "the company". Your role in your résumé is to take the hero – the company struggling with a challenge – and elevate it to a new level of performance. The reader will likely empathize with the challenges your past employers have faced and envision you as the person who can solve similar challenges for their company.

The hook: Film director Garry Marshall said he can predict the box office success of a film by standing outside the theatre as audiences exit. If people are repeating lines from the movie, it will be a hit. Why? Because they have an easy way of remembering the movie and sharing their viewing experience with friends. In your story-based résumé, your meaningful tag line and headlines will be like the "hook" of a song that stays with the reader, even after he or she has consumed hundreds of résumés.

How to Incorporate Your Story in a Résumé?

There are no set rules on how to incorporate storytelling into a résumé. I'm sharing the three tools I've found to give the greatest return for your efforts. For the ambitious, I'm also reviewing some final touches that can take résumé storytelling up a notch. How far you go into the rabbit hole is up to you.

First, the lens: Looking back at your career for stories without considering your target is like shopping for an outfit when you don't know if you'll need to wear it on a Caribbean vacation, to a board meeting or black tie event. You'll end up with too much material and much of it will be irrelevant.

What is your current career goal? What role are you seeking? Which industry or industries are you targeting? How large is your ideal company and what is its corporate culture like? Some roles (like accounting and sales) can cross industries fairly easily. In these cases, multiple industries could be included in the target. A few roles could be blended, such as business development and sales. If you're in doubt as to whether a particular target is too broad, err on the side of specificity. You can create separate résumés for divergent goals, but keep in mind the amount of job search time you have available given that you would be running two distinct job search campaigns.

Once you have your focus, use your own knowledge, job postings, and, possibly, informational interviews to identify the most important skills and qualities you'll need to demonstrate. It is very important that you start with yourself first. Many times hiring managers don't know what they want until they see a candidate they like, so the insights you and your close friends, family, and colleagues have about why you are perfect for your current targeted goal are usually what will set you apart from the crowd.

If you query hiring managers and pour over job entries before writing down your own thoughts about your strengths, your perception may be coloured, and you may miss out on your most marketable qualities.

This happened with a client of mine. She was a new graduate, but she'd worked in the Peace Corps and many domestic organizations. She found money where others couldn't, got flush toilets to a remote African village, helped underserved women get the resources they needed to improve their lives. She listed her strengths as grant writing, project management, client relations, etc.

What jumped out at me was that she moved mountains. If it needed to be done, she had the passion, creativity, and energy to realize it, no matter what obstacles stood in the way. Mountain moving is not an industry- or even function-specific quality. But it was the reason any non-profit would be very fortunate to have her over other candidates who could also claim knowledge about grant writing and such.

If you're having trouble identifying your best qualities, you can try a blind brand assessment such as the one from 360 Reach or a behaviour assessment such as DISC®. Quotes from these assessments can also make great endorsements because they are objective sources.

Take Action...Tell Your Story

Create Your Lens

Write down your target role, then the skills and qualities you possess that would allow you to shine in this position. This will be the lens or perspective you adopt as you do the exercises below.

Rank the qualities and skills into A, B and C groups, with A being the most important (such as mountain-moving and the role-specific skills like grant writing that are deal-breakers), B being fairly important, and C being "nice to have". Anything not ranking at least a C can be removed from the list.

No. 1 Fundamental Tool – The CAR Story: Now that you have your lens, let's get to the storytelling! Review your professional, educational, volunteer and even personal experiences for instances where you've demonstrated skills and qualities from you A and B lists.

Let other people sweat the little (but important) stuff

There are many people who are good editors and formatters, but very few who are familiar with how to incorporate a story into a résumé. Use the information and exercises here to create the strategy and content of your résumé. You can always get help from a friend or hire a proofreader, editor or designer to polish the grammar and format of your document.

Despite the example I gave of my own experience being offered a job despite an egregious typo, it's best to present the most polished image possible while incurring the least amount of stress. You'll want Word, PDF and plain-text versions of your résumé in common fonts that will show up properly on most PC and MAC setups.

Kimberly Robb Baker, Chief Career Storyteller, Movin' On Up Résumés

Chapter 11

Get Your Résumé Ready for Prime Time

"Without a compelling story, every résumé will be tossed aside, every interview will be a struggle and every networking opportunity will render you speechless."

~ Daisy Wright, Career Strategist and Author

Is your current résumé ready for "prime time"? This is not about the peak viewing time on television for which advertising rates are the highest. It refers to the less than 30 seconds that it takes a recruiter or hiring manager to make a decision about your résumé.

Consider this: The average length of a television ad is 60 seconds, much longer than the time it takes the most discerning, eagle-eyed recruiter to scan a résumé and decide if it should be tossed in the trash bin, deleted from a database or placed on the "for further review" pile.

If you think of your résumé as an ad for a product, and the buyer as a recruiter or hiring manager, how will you ensure that your résumé grabs their "prime time" attention and be given the cursory 30-second look?

The five tips below are not all-encompassing but should certainly help your résumé meet the prime time test:

Conduct a prime time test. Grab a copy of your résumé right now and review it. What's your impression? How is it packaged? Will it be noticed within that 30-second flash of time? Does it have an attention-grabbing headline? What have you included in the top-third of the document commonly referred to as "prime real estate"? Is the space dominated with a me-centred objective, or does it have an impressive value-based statement highlighting why you are uniquely qualified to fill the position? Does it have a strong value proposition?

Look for career-defining stories. As you continue your review, is the résumé saturated with career defining stories demonstrating your skills, strengths and accomplishments? Are these stories connected to the employer's buying motivators or needs? Or is it packed with statements and responsibilities directly from your job description with no accompanying results or outcomes? It is quite common for job seekers to create résumés laden with job descriptive statements when hiring managers want to see résumés laden with value. Eliminate such statements if you cannot show value. Ultimately, employers hire based on results (or value), not on what you were "responsible for..."

Weave in endorsements. Do you know you can enhance your résumé with third-party endorsements about your achievements and your capabilities? Not just any endorsement, but testimonials and recommendations from influencers in your network or comments culled from your performance appraisal. Not only do these comments tell the hiring manager that you are the "best thing since sliced bread", but statements coming from people who can attest to your abilities – your manager or former supervisor – give you credibility.

Experiment with a creative layout. Is your résumé created with one of those templates that everyone uses, or does it have a unique layout that captures the reader's attention and tempt them to want to read more? You don't have to be a graphic designer to create a nicely-laid out résumé that stands out and appeals to the reader.

Focus on value more than length. While most people prefer a two-page résumé, some recruiters say it depends on the level of the position. Executive recruiter, David Perry of Perry Martel, said, "Length doesn't matter to me, as long as it is laden with value." Another recruiter said, "A long résumé (8+ pages) is just too much, no matter how many years of experience a person has." How long is yours, and does it have relevant information that would grab the interest of a hiring manager? If it is laden with value, then length won't matter.

In a competitive job market when recruiters and hiring managers are deluged with hundreds of résumés for one position, your résumé must be ready to compete for prime time. Make sure to include several compelling stories that focus on your unique value. To get to those stories, ask yourself, "What problems did I solve?" "What legacy did I leave or am I leaving in my roles?" Only then will you be able to craft a résumé that will be ready for prime time.

Chapter 12

Inspiring Cover Letters

"Get a name, any name. By hook or by crook try to get a name."
~ Debra Wheatman, Career Coach

Straight Facts About Cover Letters

This chapter stresses the utility of a cover letter, and it doesn't matter if it is attached to the résumé, as some employers request, or it is created in the body of an email.

The importance of cover letters is often a matter of debate among hiring managers, job seekers and career coaches. It is widely accepted that 50 per cent of recruiters do not read cover letters. This begs the question: What about the other 50 per cent? Some job seekers make the mistake of not including a cover letter with their résumé – they believe the résumé is enough to convey their qualifications and interests in the position.

In fact, most employers expect you to include a customized cover letter with your résumé. It creates a strong first impression and tells them why you are the best person to fill the position. It also gives you an opportunity to answer potential questions before they are asked, for example, gaps in your employment.

Your cover letter should be one page in length, ideally made up of four paragraphs. Don't be tempted to make it longer, regardless of how much experience you have. As mentioned above, many recruiters don't read cover letters, and those who do, just don't have the time to read more than one page. This is one time when you can safely assume that "less is more".

- The **first** paragraph answers the "how" and "why": how you heard about the position and why you are the perfect candidate for the role. If your application is an unsolicited one, indicate that the company is your main target and that you are exploring possible opportunities.

- The **second** paragraph describes your skills, education, and experience and how your experience meets the company's needs. It also shows how they align with the position and what the employer can expect from you.

- The **third** paragraph describes your key contributions and tells stories of your achievements – how well you did what you were asked to do –and what makes you uniquely qualified for the job.

- The **fourth** paragraph is a "Call to Action" – reiterating your interest in the position, and indicating that you will be following up with them.

Some job seekers state in their cover letters that they will be following up the application with a call on a particular date. This action may appear presumptuous, but it has worked in some cases. Having said that, some job advertisements specifically say "do not call". In such cases, adhere to those requests.

How to Address Your Cover Letter

When writing your cover letter, remember that companies are like people. They like to know that you took the time to find out who they are, where they are located and who should receive your application.

You should not send a cover letter that says *To Whom It May Concern* or *Dear Sir/Madam.* It is expected that you will address the letter to someone, most likely the person who can hire you. With the availability of social media tools like LinkedIn, Facebook, Google and Twitter, it is very easy these days to find the names of people inside a company.

If a name is not given in the job posting, and you have tried to obtain a name without success, you may address the letter as *Dear Human Resources Officer, Dear Hiring Manager, Dear Hiring or Search Committee, or Director of* (fill in appropriate department or title).

How to Create an Email Cover Note

As mentioned above, some recruiters do not read cover letters. However, most will open and read an email, especially when it has a strong subject line. This section gives tips on how you can turn your email message into a captivating cover note. Essentially, it contains elements of a regular cover letter, but it is clear and concise:

- Use a strong subject line that grabs attention. Most appropriate would be the title of the position and/or the competition number.
- Use three short paragraphs to summarize why you are the best candidate for the job. Make sure it is appealing enough to convince the recruiter your résumé should be placed on the "must contact" file.
- Create a professional email signature with your contact information. This is very important as it makes it easy for recruiters to contact you. Include your name, title (if you have one), your telephone and mobile numbers.

Be Daring With Your Cover Letter

The whole point of this book is for you to do unconventional things to stand out and catch the employer's attention. Why not try something daring with your cover letter? The following are examples used by some of my clients:

Start with a question. Not any question, but one with facts that will jolt them:

Example: *Are you looking for an operations director who made one suggestion that saved a company $750,000 within six months?*

This is enough to get the attention and encourage the reader to set aside your résumé for the "must contact" file.

Tell a story that relates to your career path. Insert a good story at the beginning of your cover letter, and it doesn't have to start with "Once Upon a Time".

Example: *As I grew up, I watched my aunt, a medical doctor, treat patients, many of whom had acute cases of asthma. I saw her write prescriptions, conduct school health checkups, suture wounds and alleviate the mental and physical pain suffered by women. I decided at a very young age that I would become a health care advocate for women.*

Use a quote that demonstrates who you are. It is said that a picture tells a thousand words. Well, a quote does the same, in my opinion.

Example: *Colin Powell, Retired Colonel and former Secretary of State, said in a speech that "Excellence is not an exception, it is a prevailing attitude." As you review my career progression, you will immediately see this quote reflected in each of my roles.*

Act as if you are already there. Immaculée Ilibagiza, survivor of the Rwandan genocide, said in her book **Left to Tell**, that, not only did she envision herself sitting at her desk at the United Nations, but she wrote her name and telephone extension in the back of the UN's phone book.

Example: *My entire career has prepared me to become your next Executive Assistant. Having been the main minute-taker at the company's board meetings, I am confident I will be able to fulfil that role when I come on board.*

Daring…Yes! Impossible…No!

Chapter 13

Creating a Biography

By Audrey Prenzel, BA, BEd, CARW, CEIC

"Always live your life with your biography in mind."
~ Marisha Pessl, Author

Nothing tells a story better than a biography. It's one of the few pieces where we write about us and control the slant and tone of the content. I always suggest writing every word with the "end product" in mind. Keep it focused on ONLY what you want the reader to know about you. Depending on the purpose of the bio, you will want to target the key elements that tell the story you want to share.

So who needs a bio anyway? The answer is everyone. Here's why:

- With the ever-shrinking duration of employment periods due to downsizing, closures and off-shoring, nothing is guaranteed or permanent. This results in looking for work more often, whether it's permanent or contract. A professional bio should be part of every working person's career management toolkit.
- If you are unemployed, a bio is another marketing tool that makes sense to use. Think of **everybody** as your competition. Let's face it: any job posted anywhere online means anybody from anywhere can apply for it if they are willing to relocate. As more people realize that relocation is the new normal, this heightens the level of competition.
- It's not all about the résumé. Of course we all need an impact-rich résumé, but every once in a while, a hiring authority asks

for some other material, such as a bio, to provide an alternative perspective of an applicant as they wade through a pool of candidates. This spans entry to senior level roles.

- If you are bidding (or if you are a subcontractor of a bidder) for a government or private sector contract, a biography of each project member is frequently asked for as part of the proposal package.
- To be considered for corporate, non-governmental organization or public board of director appointments, a biography is typically requested. These can be used afterwards for public and stakeholder information.
- Various committees ask for biographies to gauge member suitability during the screening and selection phase. The bios can be re-purposed afterwards to share publicly the committee's mandate and each member's background.
- High-profile, senior-level executives and political figures have biographies for usage on websites and for introductions at speaking engagements.
- Self-employed professionals benefit from having a value-building bio to explain services and share credentials. When crafted with the right emphasis, these entice potential clients to give them a call.
- Most online networking sites provide space for a bio. It's a smart idea to have your bio scalable so it's available from a full page to 160 characters.

Let's think about what should go in your biography. The possibilities are endless, but some areas are more suited than others. Here is a cross-section of possible elements for inclusion:

- Career History
- Service or Business Overview
- Certifications/Education
- Languages Spoken
- Professional Memberships

- Committee and Board Appointments
- Publications
- Media Exposure and Interviews
- Trademarks/Patents/Inventions
- Industry/Trade Achievements
- Speaking Engagements
- Volunteer Initiatives
- Sports Involvement
- Hobbies
- Something Unexpected or Interesting

There is no need to "bare it all". To construct your own biography, identify the top five points you want others to know about you. If you are a service provider, write with the customer in mind. If you are a mid-level professional looking for a more progressive role, write with an HR screening panel in mind. If you are on track to give presentations, then write with conference speaker selection officials in mind. Let's look at some pointers to craft your story your way.

Photograph: Three words: **keep it real**. If you are an executive, having a formal pose in a conservative business suit is not only fine, it's preferable. If you are an outdoor type person, looking for an environmental sort of role, a shot in the canoe is a great idea. A pose in a classroom makes sense for teachers. The courtroom is the ideal backdrop for lawyers. A veterinarian sporting the white lab jacket petting a dog on the examination table is perfect. If you are a member of the Canadian Forces, why not be in uniform? And you don't have to pay big bucks. With high-quality digital personal cameras available these days, having a friend take the shot is perfectly acceptable.

Visual branding: The look and feel your bio projects is just as important as the content. It's no surprise that word documents with plain text simply look like word documents with plain text. To be clear, PLAIN = BORING! Make use of colour, different fonts, slogans, logos and other graphic elements that truly represent who you are. Some parts may lend themselves to bullets and text that is centred, bolded or italicized. Isolate content in text boxes. Make them pop with coloured borders. Invite the reader to engage with you by having your personal website or social media links added into the mix. An embedded video or audio recording of you telling the reader about your career journey is an ideal way to share your story.

Contact information: It doesn't sound like a big deal but if the purpose of a bio is to generate interest for others to learn more about you, shouldn't you make it easy for them? A simple phone number and email will do.

Writing tone: This is probably the most important element of a biography. If you think of your biography as a living document, the vigour of your writing will breathe life right into it. Avoid the stuffy, over-used clichés and content. Here's a tip... tack something that is potentially boring onto something else that underscores your value proposition to help tie all the points together. For example, Kaley the real estate agent was born in Toronto. On her bio she wrote: *"Kaley was born in Toronto, Ontario".* Although this is true it isn't very captivating is it? Consider this revised phrasing: *"Since Kaley has lived in Toronto her entire life, knowing the pulse of the City's real estate market is second nature to her."* Kaley now allows the reader to make the connection that she knows the nuances involved with Toronto real estate because she comes from there.

For further inspiration, I'll share with you that Kaley is bilingual. So, being a logical person, she wrote: *"Kaley is bilingual".* Not only is this boring, but the reader cannot tell what other languages she speaks. She also needed to build value by sharing this in terms of how it benefits her employer. *"Fluent in French, Kaley has been relied upon to translate for Francophones and ESL clients for the firm"* packs a lot more punch than the first sentence.

Don't dwell on the past. Nothing undermines what you are doing now than over-emphasizing what you used to do. When I first examined Kaley's bio, she wrote *"Kaley has worked at Sunshine Real Estate Ltd for 10 years. Earlier, she worked for the City Central (2 yrs), Maple Grove (3 yrs), Manchester (1 yr) and Green Lane Real Estate (4 yrs) firms where she learned how to represent both buyers and sellers fairly."* This is too much emphasis on showcasing the names of former firms. We rejigged it to read: *"Kaley honed her ability to meet the most discerning of client's needs by working at Sunshine Real Estate for the past 10 years, and at other client-centric firms within the Greater Toronto Area for the previous decade."*

As much as your biography should be a good representative of who you are, and might include some personal information, there is a boundary as to how much personal information is included. In Kaley's example, she wrote: *"Kaley is married to Barry and has a son named Ben and a daughter named Elise"*. This does not add to her value, but more specifically, it does not have anything to do with her ability to sell real estate. So, we removed it completely.

And when it came to listing her hobbies, we excluded that as well. She included everything from kayaking to singing in her church choir. Showing community and volunteer involvement makes more sense for a sales role such as real estate so we wrote: *"Kaley is an active member of the Chamber of Commerce and Big Sisters"*. This approach makes for better, more meaningful content.

Something unexpected: Who doesn't like a surprise? When we take the time to share a little something that is a bit out of the ordinary, we stand out from the crowd. I've had clients who have climbed Mount Everest, flown the Queen of England in planes, advised presidents and prime ministers, launched spacecraft and demonstrated spectacular acts of heroism. I also have clients who have never missed a day of work in the factory 20 years, started from ground zero to create thriving charities and volunteered to rebuild schools and orphanages in war-torn countries. The point is that everybody, regardless of work history, education, income, looks or geographical location, has something unique to offer.

In Kaley's case, I noticed that she uses sign language to communicate with her daughter who was born severely hearing impaired. Kaley and her husband have used American Sign Language (ASL) since their daughter's birth. I asked if she ever used sign language to communicate with clients and she said "yes". Wow! What a wonderful skill and what a shame to NOT include that in her bio. Thus: *"Kaley's ability to use ASL has eased the sales and purchase process for those clients who are deaf and hard of hearing"* was added after we mentioned her ability to speak French.

Building a biography is more strategy than anything. Share your story by planning who you want to impress and then keep your eye on that target every step of the way.

Let's look at the "before" and "after" bio versions:

Before:

Kaley Smith was born in Toronto, Ontario. Kaley has worked at Sunshine Real Estate Ltd for 10 years. Earlier, she worked as a results oriented sales rep for the City Central (2 yrs), Maple Grove (3 yrs), Manchester (1 yr) and Green Lane Real Estate (4 yrs) firms where she learned how to represent both buyers and sellers fairly. Always results oriented, Kaley is number one in her office for sales.

Kaley is married to Barry and has a son named Kevin and a daughter named Elise.

In her spare time, she enjoys kayaking, knitting, yoga, calligraphy, collecting antiques and singing in her church choir.
Contact Kaley at 555.555.5555

After:

Email: Kaley@isp.com

Cell: 555.555.5555

LI: www.linkedin.com/Kaley

Buying a home is the most important financial commitment and lifestyle decision anybody will make. It's Kaley Smith's mandate to help clients find the best home for their specific needs.

A 24-7, full-throttle approach has paved the way for Kaley to connect the right buyer with the right seller. For the benefit of sellers she strategically prices homes to secure optimal results. Further, she takes an active role in adding value to a home by launching pre-sale preparations with her hand-picked team of professionals and trades crews. Enticingly written newspaper ads, colourful information sheets, and numerous open houses are all part of the campaign. She routinely leverages a host of Internet applications to ease the buyer's search, and to gain market-dominating exposure for those who list properties with her.

Since Kaley has lived in Toronto her entire life, knowing the pulse of the City's real estate market is second nature to her. She balances relentless drive and diligence with effective listening and a helpful nature. Kaley is recognized for being attentive and patient, and never pushy.

Kaley honed her ability to meet the most discerning of client's needs by working at Sunshine Real Estate for the past 10 years, and at other client-centric firms within the Greater Toronto Area for the previous decade. For the past five years, she has been number one for sales in her office.

Fluent in French, Kaley has been relied upon to translate for Francophones and ESL clients for the firm. Kaley's ability to use ASL has eased the sales and purchase process for those clients who are deaf and hard of hearing.

In her spare time, Kaley enjoys contributing back to the community. She is an active member of the Chamber of Commerce and Big Sisters.

If you would like to learn more about how Kaley can ease your search or sell your home, give her a call. You'll join countless others who already know her dedication and passion to serve motivated home buyers and sellers are second to none.

Audrey Prenzel, Founder, Résumé Resources

Chapter 14

Preparing a Job Proposal

"A story illustrates a problem or a challenge; proposes a solution, and builds a bridge to brighter future."

~ Doug Stevenson, Story Theatre

Did you know you can create a job proposal for your ideal job even if the company has not yet realized that such a position exists? If you have done everything you could to get the attention of someone in a company and you have not been successful, then it's time to change your strategy and create a job proposal: a document that is laden with convincing stories to catch the attention of decision makers, and get them interested in you.

A job proposal is similar to, but is not, a résumé. It shows a potential employer what you can offer and why it will benefit them to hire you. According to Patrick G. Riley, author of **The One Page Proposal,** *"A job proposal enables you to showcase to employers your unique experiences, knowledge, and ideas that will make you an asset to their company. It will help you stand out, give recruiters a stronger reason to contact you, and improve your chances of getting the job you really want – all in one page."*

The job proposal involves in depth research to uncover specific problems that a company faces, then offers ideas on how to solve those problems. Not only that, but you, the job seeker, need to find out who the key decision makers are so you can address them directly. As much as HR plays a huge role in the selection process, this project is not for the HR department.

A job proposal puts you at an advantage when contacting an employer. It addresses how you would approach the challenges of the job; allows you to see yourself in the role doing exactly what you proposed to do; it makes you more appealing to recruiters; it gives you an edge in the interview, and puts you ahead of your competitors.

Here are six steps to creating a job proposal:

1. **What is it that you are good at?**
   Consider your specialty. What unique skill or expertise do you have to offer an employer? What "promise of value" can you make to an employer? Think of how your skills, experiences, abilities and work preferences will consolidate and allow you to do work you really love.

2. **Create a list of potential employers**
   This step is the start of the research phase. Once you have decided what you have to offer, develop a list of at least 10 potential employers that could benefit from your expertise. Explore websites, online profiles of companies, boards of trade, chambers of commerce, trade journals, the library, job boards (to see which companies are hiring), and other relevant sources.

3. **Schedule informational meetings**
   This is the time to take the bull by the horn and do something you may find uncomfortable – cold calling! Find people inside and outside of your targeted companies to interview to get in-depth information about their needs. Visit the companies' websites, conduct Google searches to see what else comes up about them, find former employees, and even contractors who have worked with them. Your aim is to find their pain points – where they are hurting, then eventually propose a solution.

4. **Decide on a project or service for each prospect**
   Depending on the problems or pain points you have discovered at each of your targeted employer, you should assess your skills to see where you could add value. Begin a draft outline of your strategy on how you propose to meet their needs.

5. **Develop your job proposal**
   You now have all the information you need to develop your job proposal. Use the same CAR (or PAR) approach as you would in an interview. State the **C**hallenge (or **P**roblem) you discovered, the **A**ctions you would take, and the proposed **R**esults or outcomes. You will need to tell a story, or two, to convince the employer that you understand their needs and you have a solution.

Write a Value Proposition Letter

This is not mandatory, but it could separate you from your competitors. A value proposition letter is clear, concise and compelling, and should be no longer than 150 words. It summarizes the research you have done, what you uncovered and how you could solve the problem(s).

Chapter 15

Interviewing Strategies

> *"Always remember: You're braver than you believe, stronger than you seem, and smarter than you think."*
>
> ~ A.A. Milne, English Author

Many people feel uneasy talking about themselves and are reluctant to tell their personal or on-the-job success stories. Modesty has its place, but not in the interview. If you don't know how to tell compelling stories during interviews, you may miss out on an opportunity for a job or a promotion.

Some recruiters and employers report that although most candidates tell a great story on paper, when they are invited for interviews they fail on their soft skills. They struggle to articulate their stories. The main reason for this is that they do not understand what the employer is looking for and, even if they do, they are not effective at telling a convincing story.

Preparing for the interview is very important and understanding the various types of interviews will help you to confidently express yourself and impress the interviewer.

Types of Interviews

Employers use a variety of interview methods and techniques to select candidates. Some of the more common types are:

- The telephone interview
- The traditional interview
- The panel interview
- The group interview
- The case interview
- The restaurant interview
- The behaviour-based interview
- The informational interview

The Telephone Interview: has become very popular. Many employers use it to screen candidates; that is, you might be asked a few questions, most of which will relate to what's on your résumé. Depending on your answers and the way in which you handle yourself, you may or may not be invited to an in-person interview.

Treat a telephone interview as if it's in-person. Have your résumé, note pad and a pen handy; get yourself mentally prepared, and find a quiet place where you can talk. During the call, sit up straight, concentrate and have a pleasant smile on your face. Listeners can hear it in your voice if you are feeling flustered or tired!

As someone actively searching for a job, you should be prepared at all times. If you do receive a call and are asked to be interviewed on the spot, it is okay for you to ask to call the reviewer back in a few minutes. This gives you time to gather everything and get to a spot where you won't be disturbed.

The Traditional Interview: is the most common of all the interviews where you will be asked questions such as: Tell me about yourself? What are your strengths and weaknesses? Why do you think you are the best person for the job? Do you have experience in this type of work? With these questions, it is very easy to give answers that you believe the interviewer wants to hear.

Short answers do not give the interviewer much opportunity to ask follow-up questions. Many hiring mistakes have been made with this type of interview, so employers are moving away from traditional interviewing and often will combine that style with what is known as behaviour-based interviews. These will be discussed in detail later.

The Panel Interview: means you are going to be interviewed by a number of people at the same time. This is usually an overwhelming experience as you are getting questions from different people and it's a bit harder to focus. The important point is to treat each interviewer with equal respect. However, you will want to address the interviewer who has asked the question you are answering, while scanning the faces of the other panellists.

The Group Interview: is a bit different from the panel interview. You may have one or more interviewers, but candidates are interviewed in groups. This is one way of determining how you measure up to each other in terms of your confidence, ability to communicate or how comfortable you are working in a team environment. While you would want to impress the interviewer(s) it is not the time to criticize or show up any weaknesses in the other candidates.

The Case Interview: is becoming more prevalent these days and it's chiefly given to MBA candidates or someone engaged in consulting. The interviewer wants to know the steps you would take to solve a particular problem. He or she then observes your problem-solving skills and listens to how you answer the questions.

The Restaurant Interview: if you are ever asked to attend an interview at a restaurant, don't consider it a strange request. While the majority of interviews are done in an office, some recruiters may decide to interview you at a restaurant. This act is not meant to intimidate you or to assess your table manners. It is more to meet with you in a more relaxed and less formal atmosphere.

Having said that, it may be a more relaxed environment for the interviewer, but a tensed one for you because the same interview rules apply. Treat it as if you were being interviewed in an office.

Arrive early, dress appropriately and make sure you have done your research on the company. Know the location of the restaurant, even if that means going there a day or two prior to your interview. In addition, be polite to the restaurant staff, turn off your cell phone, do not order any alcoholic drink even if invited to do so, select a reasonably-priced meal, listen carefully and, most of all, be prepared to answer and ask the right questions.

The Informational Interview: provides opportunities to hear some great (and sometimes not too great) stories. They open the door to hear stories of other people's career paths, provide ways to start building or expand our networks; they help to build self-confidence and help job seekers prepare for interviews

The Behaviour-Based Interview: is quite popular with employers because it focuses on how you perform on the job. It is, therefore, absolutely necessary that you prepare very well for this type of interview. A behaviour-based interview is like storytelling. It will require you to recall specific experiences that demonstrate the competencies set out in the job posting. The employer will be looking for specific job-related examples of skills you used and results you accomplished.

The idea behind the behavioural interview is that your past performance can determine your future performance. If you performed well with a given task or in a given role, it is assumed you will do the same in a similar situation. Bear in mind that this type of interview also measures your ability to deal with adverse or bad situations, so it's okay to recall instances when things did not go well. The employer wants to know how you handled the situation and what lessons you learned.

You will be able to identify a behaviour-based interview when the question begins with "Tell me a time when…";"Give me an example of…";"Describe a situation where…."

Behaviour-based interviews are usually about competencies – the skills, knowledge and attributes that the employer has already decided a candidate should have to be successful in the position. Some common competencies would include skills in communication, leadership, adaptability, customer service, decision-making, problem-solving, and organizing and planning.

Tips on Preparing for the Behaviour-Based Interview

Even if you are not in a behaviour-based interview, prepare yourself for it anyway. When you understand how this type of interview works, you stand a very good chance of doing well. Here are some guidelines in preparing for a behaviour-based interview:

- Review the job posting and identify the competencies – the knowledge, skills and attributes – that are requested.
- Develop at least four stories for each competency.
- Reflect on your job performances and recall problems or challenges that you encountered. Develop stories around those problems. What action(s) did you take to solve the problem and what were the results? What happened as a result of your actions?
- The acronyms PAR (Problem, Action, Results), SAR (Situation, Action, Results) or CAR (Challenge, Action, Results) can be used as guides when answering the questions.
- This type of interview asks for specific answers, not hypothetical ones. This is to make sure that you are not making up the stories as you go along.

- Don't be surprised if some interviewers ask for proof of your stories. Who else worked on the project with you? Can they call to verify your role in the project?
- Incorporate behavioural interview techniques into your answers even if you are asked traditional interview questions and distinguish yourself from other candidates.

Tips on Preparing for Informational Interviews

- Identify and research companies by using the Internet, yellow pages, contacts in your network, newspaper, industry directories and trade journals.
- Identify a person within a company who is in your field of work and with whom you wish to speak.
- Make an appointment by email, letter or by telephone.
- Make it clear that you are asking for information only.
- Prepare questions for the meeting.
- Dress appropriately.
- Begin the information meeting by thanking the person for taking the time to speak with you.
- Listen carefully, and seek the person's permission if you wish to take notes.
- Do not prolong the meeting beyond the time you requested.
- Express thanks and end the meeting.
- Follow up with a thank-you letter.
- Keep in touch with your contact.

Sample Script for an Informational Interview

"Hello______, I was speaking with ____________, and s/he suggested that I give you a call. I am currently a ___________ and am curious about the roles of people currently working in the field. I was wondering if you would be able to meet with me for 15-20 minutes to talk about your role and the organization you work for."

If they are too busy, you could ask when would be a convenient time to call back, or if they could suggest someone else who might be able to speak with you. Follow that up by asking for a telephone number and if you could use their name when you call.

When you actually meet with an individual, introduce yourself and thank him/her for taking the time to talk or meet with you. Tell them your story – enough about yourself (interests and skills) – so that they can offer you relevant information. Remember, it's not all about you. You should also be listening to their stories. The following are suggested questions to ask. You can also customize them to suit your situation:

- What aspects of this job gives you the most satisfaction?
- Tell me how you got into this line of work?
- What skills and qualities are necessary to do your job well?
- How long have you worked for this organization?
- What are your major responsibilities?
- Who is your immediate supervisor? What is his/her title?
- What do you perceive to be the major rewards of this job?
- What are the major frustrations in this job?
- What do you like most about this job?
- What are the most frequently recurring problems?
- Have your duties changed within the last few years, months?
- What advice would you give to a person coming into a company like this?

- My strongest skills are______________. Do you know of any other company that could use someone with my skills?
- Would you have another name or two you could refer me to who could give me additional information about this occupation?

Case Study: The Value of Informational Interviews

In mentoring one of my clients in her job search as well as a member of Toastmasters, I encouraged her to conduct informational interviews to hear people's stories and also build her professional network. After she had had several of these meetings, she sent me the following update:

"I am so grateful you suggested I conduct informational interviews. It was a new strategy for me, and, while I was nervous, I put my fears aside and embarked on a new adventure.

With your encouragement, and help in customizing the script that you gave me, I contacted the economic director at one of our cities. My script was so effective that the director replied as follows:

"Thank you, ______, for your kind note. Much appreciated!

I would be happy to spend 15-20 minutes with you as you requested. Let me know when you will be visiting the city, and I will make arrangements to meet you."

At the end of our discussion, the director advised me to contact the event planner for the local Chamber of Commerce. That informational interview was magnificent. She was happy to know that you have been my mentor in Toastmasters and in my job search.

I arrived at her office at 9:22 a.m. and she was already there. She asked about me and my family, and why we moved to Canada. I asked her many of the questions you and I discussed. We had a good conversation. Every now and again, I would ask her if I needed to wind up quickly, but she insisted that we continue the conversation.

To my surprise, she enthusiastically introduced me to several officials who were visiting her office that day. These individuals were from various industries – banking, insurance, staffing and academia. In fact, I was introduced to eight people. She suggested I arrange informational interviews with all of them and to use her as a reference. I took their business cards and promised to follow up.

My next meeting was with the president of the Business Development Corporation. I had visited his LinkedIn profile before meeting him, and he was surprised that I did the research and found out about him.

At the end of our meeting, he said he would try to connect me with some big bank officials who could give me additional guidance. He also commented that conducting informational interviews was "very smart work", and it is something I could teach others to do.

Another meeting was with the support services coordinator at one Canadian university. We had a very warm conversation that went on for more than an hour.

She made me feel very comfortable and I learned a lot as she shared her journey and experiences over the years. As a former university professor, I was eager to hear if there were potential opportunities for me to teach in a Canadian university.

This process gave me the confidence I needed to advance my career. I was recently hired as a part-time professor at one of the major colleges in Canada, teaching my specialization – macroeconomics. I am teaching part-time at a small private college. In addition, I am enrolled in a professional development program at the Rotman School of Management, University of Toronto.

My conclusion is that asking for informational interviews is a very good strategy if someone wants to land a job or advance their career. I continue to do informational interviews to build my professional network. I have found that people are willing to speak with me and share their stories. Below is a sample thank-you note I customized and sent to the individuals I met.

Dear ___________,

I know how extremely busy you are and I am very grateful that you were willing to share some time with me last week. I learned so much about your career progression and the work that you do at the ________.

It would be a privilege for me to participate in some volunteer work in any area where you believe I could use my research abilities. It would definitely be a winning situation as I would be learning something new and the organization would be benefiting from my skills.

Thank you as well for giving me the names of ______ and ____ of the _________ and the ________. I will definitely be sending them an email in the next few days. I also appreciate that you suggested I use your name when contacting them.

Again I want to thank you for your time, and hope I can keep in touch with you.

Sincerely,

____

Chapter 16

Ten Most Challenging Job Interview Questions

By Carole Martin

"There is no greater agony than bearing an untold story inside you."
~ Maya Angelou, American Author, Poet

There is no way of predicting which questions will be asked in an interview, but by reviewing the most common questions you will begin to focus on how to present yourself in the most prepared and positive manner.

1. **Tell me about yourself**

   Any conversation in which one person is getting to know another person starts with the question, "Tell me about yourself?" Whether it is in a job interview, in a media interview, a social setting, a sales call, a chance meeting with someone – this question will be asked in one way or another.

   The words, "Tell me about yourself" may not be the exact words used - but the question will be there. "What do you do?" "Tell us about your background." Basically, "Who are you?"

   Be able to articulate what you have to offer – particularly as a match for the requirements of the job. Give them a summary of your skills, experience and your strengths. Tell them who you are in two to four minutes – depending on the circumstances.

2. **Why has it taken you so long to find a job? (This may be asked in different ways to find out what you've been doing since your last job.)**
   It's amazing that employers are still asking this type of question. Don't they read what's going on in the job market? If they were informed, they would know the answer to that question is: "Jobs are very scarce right now and unemployment is at an all-time high."

   So what is the correct answer to give when you're asked such a question in an interview? There is no "correct" answer. However, a technique that may work is to take the focus off the length of your job search and to move the focus to what you have to offer.

3. **What is your greatest weakness?**
   The most dreaded question of all. Handle this question by minimizing the weakness and emphasizing the strengths. Stay away from personal qualities and concentrate on professional traits.

   There is a formula for difficult questions called the *Sandwich Technique*.

   (+) Begin with a positive statement
   (–) Slip in the negative (or weakness)
   (+) End with a positive statement

   Example:
   "I am always working on improving my communication skills to be a more effective presenter. I take every opportunity to practice speaking before groups and I recently joined Toastmasters which I find very helpful."

4. **Why should we hire you?**
   Prepare and know your product – YOU! Summarize your experiences: *"With five years experience working in the financial industry, and my proven record of saving the company money, I could make a*

big difference in your company. I am known for my ability to find contacts and build long-lasting relationships. I am confident I would be a great addition to your team."

5. **Why do you want to work here? OR What attracts you to this job?**

   The interviewer is listening for an answer that indicates you've given this some thought, and are not just sending out résumés because there is an opening. Doing research should give you plenty of reasons why you want to work there.

   Example:

   "I've been searching for a company with the specific mission of helping people to get jobs. When I came across your position and began to research the company's goals and accomplishments, I knew that this is where I wanted to work. I want to make a difference and feel good about my job and contribution to the company and to helping people."

6. **Why did you leave (are leaving) your job?**

   This question is almost a certainty. If you are unemployed, put your leaving in a positive context: *"I managed to survive two downsizings, but the third round was a 20 per cent reduction in the workforce, which included me. I really liked my job and want to find one similar to what I was doing at my last company."*

   If you are employed, focus on what you want in your next job: *"After two years, I made the decision to look for a company that is more inline with the goals I have set for myself – mainly to get into customer service management. I know that I now have something to offer through my experiences and education."*

7. **What are your goals?**

   Why would the employer want to know this? Basically they want to know how long you're going to "stick around". This is a bit tricky because you may be taking a job to survive at this time. When the economy improves you will be looking for something more in line with your goals.

Be careful not to convey this message if that is what you are doing. Be honest but state your goals in the short term and long term.

Example
"You might say that I am stepping back to go forward. I believe that it is easy to lose touch with the bigger picture and I see this as an opportunity to do something different than what I have been doing. Long term I would like to assume more responsibility and move up in the organization if possible."

8. **What would you do if you had to deal with an angry customer (or use a situation that the job you are going for would be likely to be concerned about)**
This is a situational question and what the interviewer is looking for is your thinking process. Situational questions are difficult to prepare for because they can be about any imaginable situation.

   If you think about it you have a natural way of solving problems – one that is yours. You automatically go through steps, whether you realize it or not. State these steps.

9. **Tell me about a time when... or Describe a situation when...(you had to deal with an angry customer or something that the job you are interviewing for would be concerned about)**
This type of question is a behavioural question. The interviewer wants to hear about your past behaviour – good and bad. If you did it before chances are that you can do it again. The best way to prepare for this type of question is with "a story".

Like all stories, it should include a beginning, a middle and an end. The problem occurs with the proportions of the story. Most people focus on the beginning, skimp on the middle, and forget the ending entirely. It is extremely important that you have proof to back whatever you declare in the interview.

10. What salary are you seeking?

The first rule of salary negotiation is to be prepared with your numbers – your needs. You need to know what you want. You never want to be caught off-guard. When they ask you questions about salary you want to be prepared and ready with answers.

You have several options.

- You can tell them what you were making at your last job. (Not recommended if you can avoid revealing this information).
- You can give them a range that is acceptable to you – making sure that the lowest number is enough to cover your basic needs. (Better way of handling this difficult question).
- You can postpone the discussion until you have more facts about the company and the entire package. (If possible this is the best scenario for you. Only then will you be able to do a fair comparison of what you have made in the past; satisfy your own basic needs; and get the deal that is the best for you).

There is no right or wrong answer, but how you handle this discussion will be key to your ability to negotiate a high offer.

Carole Martin is the President of The Interview Coach

Chapter 17

Honesty Is the Best Policy

By John Ribeiro

> *"Honesty is the first chapter in the book of wisdom."*
> ~Thomas Jefferson, Third President of the USA

As a manager of an internal technical help desk, I have had the opportunity to interview many candidates. In the span of four years I interviewed approximately 70 individuals, and within five minutes I am able to tell whether the person was sincere and if they would be a good fit for the team.

Even though I was looking for someone with a strong technical background, that was not the most important characteristic. As it is often said, most new employees fail not because of their technical abilities, but because of their soft skills. From my perspective, having someone who was honest, straightforward and dedicated always won me over. The sincerity would come through the responses, both verbal and nonverbal.

One candidate I interviewed some time ago really stood out and it was because of his sincerity and honesty. I asked him, "What was the most important thing in your life at this time?" He responded that it was his family.

This was quite the response. In previous interviews, candidates would usually respond with career, growing inside the organization or becoming a better technical support technician. But when he responded with "family", it really caught my attention. Not only was it different, but it also gave me a sense that the interviewee was dedicated. Out of curiosity, I asked the candidate to expand on what he meant. He explained that he was looking for stability and wanted to provide for his family.

He was a new immigrant and in his country of origin, good and stable job opportunities were not available for everyone. In moving to Canada he knew that he could give his family a different and better life. What really stood out was the way he delivered his response. It was honest, sincere and passionate. I knew immediately that I wanted this person on my team, and I felt he was really going to give it 110 per cent.

As a manager and a person who enjoys building teams, people who speak from the heart will always get the job over those who give standard and generic responses.

John Ribeiro is Manager of Process Automation, Rogers Communications Inc.

Chapter 18

How to Read an Interviewer's Mind

> *"I can't go back to yesterday – because I was a different person then"*
>
> ~ Lewis Carroll, English Author

The main reason job seekers fear and fail at interviews is that they are attempting to read the interviewer's mind then give answers they think the interviewer wants to hear. This mind-guessing game will not work and is destined to fail.

This is where a good understanding of the PAR/CAR/SAR interview concept will be helpful to the job seeker. If he or she knows how to develop success stories, demonstrating **challenges** faced, **actions** taken and **results** obtained, it puts them in a better position to ace the interview.

Below are five randomly selected questions, each of which includes a sneak peek into the mind of the interviewer as well as strategies on how to answer the questions:

Q1: Why should I consider you a strong applicant for this position? What have been your most significant achievements in your previous job?

What the interviewer wants to know: Does this candidate understand the duties and responsibilities associated with this position? Does he have the specific skills, abilities and the right experience that demonstrate a high level of proficiency?

Strategy: From your review of the job posting, you would have identified the skills and knowledge that are critical to the position. Offer your specific achievements that directly or closely relate to the job.

Q2: What were three of your most significant accomplishments in your previous role that directly relate to the position we are discussing today?

What the interviewer wants to know: Is the candidate aware of the contributions she has made to the employer? Has she left a legacy that has had significant impact on the company? Did she make or save the company money?

Strategy: Recall and tell stories of instances where your efforts made significant impact on the company's bottom line and where you saved the company time or money. Also mention any awards or recognitions you received for your efforts.

Q3: If I were to contact your supervisor, what would she say about your ability to complete a difficult task? What criticism would she have about your technical competence?

What the interviewer wants to know: Is the candidate someone who accepts or resists management directives? Does he have a good work ethic? Does he willingly pitch in to help co-workers with challenges?

Strategy: Focus on the teamwork/collaborative competencies that directly relate to the job for which you are interviewing. Give specific examples of how you get along with your co-workers and how willing you were to go the extra mile to get the job done.

Q4: Describe a situation when you worked with someone whose work style was different from yours. What problems did you encounter? How did you resolve the problems?

What the interviewer wants to know: Can this candidate work with different personalities? Is she accepting of others? Is she flexible? Is she aware that there's more than one way to accomplish a task?

Strategy: Offer stories that demonstrate flexibility and tact when dealing with people and problems. Relate your cross-cultural experience and your respect for diversity.

Q5: Tell me about a challenge our company is facing and offer a solution. Why do you feel this solution is the answer?

What the interviewer wants to know: Does the candidate understand our industry and can he offer some insights into potential challenges the industry is facing?

Strategy: Tell stories that demonstrate a thorough understanding of the industry and offer solutions. Give examples of ideas you offered that were accepted in your previous role. If you can do this you will be an extremely desirable candidate.

Take Action....Tell Your Story

Given what you now know about behavioural interviews and competencies, develop several stories using the CAR (**C**hallenge, **A**ction, **R**esults) format.

CHALLENGE – what was the problem?
ACTION – What actions did you take, what did you do?
RESULTS – What happened? What were the outcome(s).

This format allows you to craft a concise and convincing story that demonstrates your "fit" for the job.

- **Communication Skills**
  Describe one of the most difficult communication situations you have encountered to date. How did you prepare? What impact did this situation have on the way you communicate today?

  CHALLENGE:

  ACTION:

  RESULTS:

- **Problem Solving**
  Describe a specific situation where an unexpected problem surfaced and you had to resolve it.

  CHALLENGE:

  ACTION:

  RESULTS:

- **Team Building**
  Describe a time when you had to lead or coordinate the efforts of a group.

  CHALLENGE:

  ACTION:

  RESULTS:

- **Organizing & Planning**
  Describe how you deal with unexpected events on the job.

  CHALLENGE:

  ACTION:

  RESULTS:

- **Decision Making**
  Tell me about a difficult decision you made at work.

  CHALLENGE:

  ACTION:

  RESULTS:

Chapter 19

Working With Recruiters

> *"When you are looking for a job, think outside the box. Do something impressive. Do something different. Do something that will stand out."*
>
> ~ Will Thomson, Recruiter

Many job seekers believe that the job search is all about the résumé and cover letter, but often they are not aware of who they are, what they're selling and what recruiters want to buy. Instead of taking the time to thoughtfully recall their success stories, create a professional résumé and engage with recruiters, they hurriedly write a sub-par résumé, submit it through an application tracking system, then passively wait to be contacted. When they fail to get a response, they talk about how difficult it is to find a job.

In an article carried on the website *Bulls Eye Recruiting* titled **How to Impress a Recruiter**, recruiter Will Thomson told the story of a young graduate who impressed him by the way he reached out to him. The young man went to LinkedIn, researched Thomson's profile, found his Twitter handle, and sent him a tweet when he found out he was hiring for a position that he was interested in. According to Thomson: "He instantly separated himself from the pack by doing something different."

Similarly, Sandy Khan, the global recruiter mentioned earlier in the book, said that "job candidates must learn the art of storytelling if their wish is to be hired by their target companies...You must learn to articulate your stories to recruiters and hiring managers and these stories should demonstrate your capabilities and potential."

Recruiters understand what employers are looking for. They know that the traditional mode of applying for jobs do not work. This is what I teach my clients – that they cannot and should not rely solely on job boards for their job search. Instead, they should use these boards as research tools. Use them to find out what companies are hiring, what skills they are looking for, and who the decision makers are at their target companies. Armed with this information, they can reach out and engage recruiters and hiring managers.

It is said that most applicant tracking systems are visible to global recruiters. If that is the case, recruiters are able to see which companies and positions candidates are applying for, and whether or not they are being rejected for roles. The more rejections these candidates get, the less attractive they will become to recruiters. Be careful, therefore, that you are not spreading yourself too thin.

The Three-Bucket Recruitment Strategy*

When working with recruiters, it is important to understand that they (recruiters) normally use a three-bucket strategy to source and select candidates.

The first bucket is for candidates who have been referred to the recruiter. These candidates will be contacted first because they are potentially best fits. The second bucket contains the names of candidates who are already in the recruiter's networks, or those they found themselves through keyword searches.

The third bucket is the big black hole. This is the recruiter's last resort, and they only go there if they haven't already found their perfect candidate in the first or second bins. Candidates likely to be lumped in this third bucket would be job board candidates. That is the reason relying solely on job boards is not the best use of your time because you won't be given priority.

The alternative is to have a completed, keyword-rich online profile, preferably LinkedIn, that will ensure your profile garners more views and potentially more opportunities.

Major Players in the Recruiting Industry

When deciding to work with recruiters (or headhunters), it makes sense to understand the recruiting industry. This section offers an inside look at the industry from an expert.

David Perry, who was mentioned earlier in the book, offered some pointers about the major players in the recruiting industry and how they function. From this information, you will determine if, when and how you should work with recruiters. The onus is on you to conduct research, interview other recruiters and arrive at your own conclusion.

The recruiting industry has two major players – firms that operate as Retainers and Contingency Agencies.

Retainer means that they get paid large sums of money to find someone with an exact fit for a specific project.

Contingency means that the recruiting firm is going to get paid if the employer hires the candidate the agency presents to them.

David explained that the challenge in sending résumés to retained search firms is similar to going to the casino and putting everything on 7 on the roulette wheel. If the marble lands on 7 and you are 7 you win. But there's a lot of other numbers and the odds are against you.

The above analogy explains why it might be better to send your résumé to a retained search firm only if they have a specific project that you are ideally suited for. If not, it could be a waste of time for you and the recruiter.

On the other hand, the contingency recruiter faces stiff competition. There is the HR department who is going to try to fill the job themselves so they won't have need for the recruiter. Then there are the other contingency recruiters working on the assignment. This recruiter has about 72 hours to get in and out of the project with a good shot of presenting a candidate who might get an interview. Only the recruiter who is successful in finding the right candidate will be paid.

The other piece to the recruiting puzzle is that if you do send your résumé to a contingency agency and they decide that they are going to market you, they don't have to tell you who you are being presented to. That becomes problematic because now when the recruiter presents your résumé to an employer, by law that recruiter has a right to be paid for up to a year if that employer hires you, whether or not hiring you had anything to do with the recruiter.

Getting a behind-the-scenes look at recruiters will help you, the job candidate, determine how best to work with them, if at all.

**Concept attributed to Sandy Khan from* Poets and Quants *link.*

Chapter 20

Crafting Your Salary Negotiation Story

"Never bargain or job hunt from a position of weakness. Soar like an eagle, even when you are feeling like a wounded pigeon."

~ George C. Fraser, Chairman and CEO, FraserNet Inc.

When it comes to salary negotiations, experts will tell you to postpone salary discussions until you have been offered the job. That does not mean you should wait until that time to craft your negotiation story.

Ask yourself:

- What's the minimum I am willing to accept?
- What is the going rate for people in my field and at my level?
- What other non-monetary benefits are being offered?

While most employers are reasonable and will compensate you fairly, be aware that some companies have a set salary range based on what they currently pay people in similar roles and what their competitors are paying. They may also have a predetermined range and will not negotiate. That's why research is important.

Here are some things to consider before accepting the offer:

- **Conduct research** to find out what the average salary and benefit packages are in other companies for people in your field. Use social media resources like LinkedIn, Facebook and Twitter to reach out to people in your network or people who are connected to them to find out what an appropriate salary would be. Review websites such as: www.salary.com, salary.monster.ca, www.payscale.com, www.careerjournal.com and www.salaryexpert.com to find salary information on many professions. Bear in mind that these figures are not universally applicable so take into consideration locations (cities, regions, provinces or territories). Having this information puts you in a better position to negotiate.

- **Take some time to review the offer**. Most times, employers expect that you will want some time to consider the offer before giving them an answer. Negotiate for more than money. Think of non-monetary benefits and perks.
- **Be firm with your expectations**, but be ready to compromise if it appears reasonable and if you sense they are doing their best.
- **Never use personal issues as a way to get a higher salary**. Focus on what you have to offer the employer.

If you have the confidence to tell a compelling negotiation story, it's an indication to the employer that you will be able to negotiate on behalf of the company, whether or not it's going to be a part of your role. Remember, it is up to you to convince the employer of the value you will bring to the organization. That makes it easier for them to accept your proposal.

While salary negotiation is usually used in conjunction with a new employee joining a company, the same process applies if you have been given a promotion or if your job responsibilities have changed. In that case, it could be referred to as "asking for a raise". To do so, you have to have a convincing story that will persuade your employer to give you the raise you believe you deserve.

Take Action...Tell Your Story

Before you start the salary negotiation dialogue:

- Consider your potential contributions to the role
- Research salary ranges for your industry or profession
- Write out a compelling narrative

Chapter 21

Selecting the Right References

> *"Always thank them, especially if you get a job. A handwritten note goes further than an email."*
>
> ~ Marty Britton, Britton Management

It is customary for employers to conduct reference and background checks on candidates they are planning to hire. This process is critical to successful hiring and is necessary to prevent dishonesty and to make sure that employers have full information on potential employees, especially because hiring is a very costly process.

In choosing people to act as references, you should make sure that they are individuals who are able to tell stories of your capabilities and accomplishments. Ideally, the referees you pick will be professionals you know through business, non-profit organizations, your church or professional associations. It is crucial to request permission to use their names in your job search or marketing material. Not only is it polite, but it ensures the individuals will be prepared for a call and will most likely speak positively about you.

It is equally important that you keep in contact with these individuals and keep them up-to-date with your progress. Once you have been invited to an interview, provide a copy of your current résumé and the job posting to your references. It allows them to have the same information as the employer. After the interview, give them an idea of how the interview went and what things were highlighted during the discussion. This will help them respond well and mention things that are relevant.

Candidate-Supplied vs Workplace References

It is important to note that different companies handle the reference process in different ways. Imagine that your impressive résumé got you the interview. You built a good rapport with the panel and you are feeling confident that you might get the job. Just as you are getting ready to pull out your reference list, someone asks you to explain your relationship with your bosses and colleagues at each of your past workplaces. Wow! That's a curve ball you were not expecting. Suddenly it seems that all that effort in alerting your references was a waste of time.

Some employers believe that this common practice of relying on "candidate-supplied super fans" is not objective. Deborah Aarts, Senior Editor at **Profit Magazine** wrote that "candidate-supplied references are usually nothing more than glowing reviews".

The chairman of an executive search firm as well as one small business owner agree with Ms Aarts that the practice is flawed because candidates are only going to give you people who'll say good things about them.

Needless to say, employers still need performance verification from people with whom you have worked. They want to make sure that you are going to be able to do the job and that you will fit in with the company's culture.

Letters of References or Direct Contacts

Letters of references are sometimes accepted, but employers still prefer to contact references directly. This is to make sure that the person does exist, and that the candidate did not make an agreement with a friend, relative or other person to "put in a good word" on their behalf.

Instead of reference letters, you could create a neat, one-page document with a list of your references. Each name should be accompanied by at least one contact method and should include some, or all, of the following details:

- Person's Name: (Mr/Ms/Dr, etc. followed by First Name Last Name)
- Title: (Manager, Business Owner, Associate, etc.)
- Place of Business: (Company/Organization Name)
- Company Address: (Full mailing address)
- Work Phone: (Business phone number, with area code plus any extension number)
- Home Phone: (Include this if they prefer being called at home)
- Email Address: (Optional, but good to provide)
- Relationship: (What this person is to you: e.g., Supervisor, Church Leader, Colleague, Employee)
- Length of Relationship: (How long have you known this person?)

When to Present Your Reference Page

If asked for your reference list during an interview, you can either present it to the interviewer immediately (if you did have a chance to alert your references), or you could respond with something like this: "I have a list, but would appreciate time to let my contacts know that you may be calling. May I send it to you tomorrow, please?"

You can enclose your reference list with your online or hardcopy thank-you letter the next day. For those rare instances where you may be concerned about your current employer's reaction, it is also fine to say that you would be delighted to supply those once a job offer has been formally made.

There are advantages to providing your reference information after the interview or, if you could, following an actual job offer:

- You may realize that much of the interview was focused on topics that would be best addressed by the person you put last on your list – or someone you forgot to include. This gives you time to rearrange the list or contact the missing individual for permission to add their information.
- You will be able to give each person on your list the courtesy of a phone call. The purpose is to let them know who may be calling and for what type of role as well as to thank them, once again, for agreeing to help.

Whether you have the opportunity to withhold your reference page or not, be sure to let those agreeing to be on the list know how much you appreciate their willingness to support you. This is a good way to show how you value them and it will help them to remember you in a most positive way in the future.

How to Handle Negative References

As a candidate, you should be ready to explain the highs and lows in each of your positions, if asked. This is not the time to badmouth the boss, ex-boss or anyone else. If the relationship was not all that great, say so, but frame it in a way that's open and honest. Something like:

"I am not sure what George at Widget Inc. would say about me at this point since he wasn't too happy when I resigned. After three years in the department, I was bypassed for a promotion and asked to train the new hire. I decided it was time to explore other opportunities and so I left for the position with ABC Company. That position represented not only a hike in salary, but the responsibilities were exactly what I was looking for. As you can see, I excelled in that role and was promoted within 12 months of joining the company."

Most employers know that people are not perfect and that work relationships sour. However, if you are willing to be transparent and authentic, and discuss the situation candidly while focusing on lessons learned, you could end up being a better reference for yourself than anyone else could.

Questions Your References May be Asked

As mentioned earlier, it is very costly to make the wrong hire. Therefore, employers look for honest answers, not only during the interview but when they contact references. The following 10 questions is a representative sample of what your references may be asked. While there are no guarantees, knowing what these questions are ahead of time will put you in a better position to advise your references on how to steer the reference process:

1. On a scale of 1-10, how would you rate the candidate?
2. Describe the candidate's day-to-day responsibilities on the job
3. What kind of situation would you not hesitate to put the candidate in? What kind of situation would give you pause?
4. Provide an example of how the candidate raises the bar for herself and for those around her.
5. If you could create the perfect work environment for the candidate, what would it look like?

6. What kind of development plan was communicated to the candidate and how did he respond?
7. How would you describe his interpersonal skills?
8. What would you say motivated her most?
9. Would you rehire the candidate?
10. Why did the candidate leave? Could the candidate have stayed if he had wanted to?

The answers to the above questions could be quite telling.

This chapter includes excerpts from Lynda Reeves' contribution to this topic in ***No Canadian Experience, Eh***

SECTION III

ADVANCING YOUR CAREER

"As we succeed and advance in our careers, we inevitably encounter situations that challenge our abilities. We also cross paths with honest critics, powerful competitors and out-and-out enemies. Running into roadblocks can cause feelings of doubt and unworthiness but it also provides opportunities for true growth."

~Joyce M. Roché, former VP at Avon,
former COO at Carson Products and
Retired President & CEO of Girls Incorporated

Chapter 22

Onboarding: Set Yourself Up for Success in Your New Job

By Sue Edwards

> *"The five steps in teaching an employee new skills are preparation, explanation, showing, observation and supervision."*
> ~ Bruce Barton, Playwright

Congratulations! You've landed a great new job. Your excitement abounds! If you are like many people, you may also have considerable anxiety. The first weeks and months in a new job are a big adjustment and, frankly, full of challenges. This article will help you to appreciate the behaviours that research has shown are important for setting yourself up for success in your new role with your new employer.

Typically, the first 90 days in a new job is considered the "onboarding timeframe": a time when you "get on board" with your new organization and learn its unique cultural nuances, figure out your boss's style and find your way around the organization. In my work as an Onboarding Coach, I am privileged to support a wide range of individuals in ramping up well in their new environments.

Here are some of the tips that I share with my clients:

Listen, observe and ask questions: Overwhelmingly line managers, human resources professionals, external coaches and recruiters alike say that the most important skills to focus on in the first 90 days in a new job are "listening, observing and asking questions". It seems so simple and yet it is difficult for people to accept.

Ironically, after all the time you've spent during the recruitment process being asked about your background, experience and focusing on whether you "have what it takes" for the role, once you are hired, the best approach is essentially to become a learner again.

In your first few weeks, it is important for you to actively seek opportunities to meet with, listen to and observe as many different people and situations as possible. This way, when you do move to action or offer your opinion, it will be grounded in the reality of your new organization.

Use the early weeks effectively and soak up as much as you can about your new environment. You will be valued more for having insightful questions in the first few weeks than for offering quick answers.

Build relationships: Building new relationships is also important for success in a new organization. While there are various relationships that are important to build, the priority focus should be on:

- Your boss
- Your peers
- Your direct reports (if your position involves supervision of others)

These relationships are critical to establishing the foundation necessary to equip yourself for both near-term and longer-term success.

It is particularly important to gain an understanding of your manager's preferred communication style and preferences for being updated. It is also critical to walk the fine line between respecting your boss's time and being pro-active about asking for information and support.

Creating a connection with peers and direct reports at a personal level helps you to enlist their support and have ready access to information.

Respect the existing culture : Even if you've been told you are being hired to "foster change" or to "challenge status quo", it is critical to **first** demonstrate interest in, and respect for, the prevailing culture, company history, business practices, etc. No one wants to hear "at my old company, we did it this way". Showing genuine interest in what your new organization does well, provoking thinking about what strengths can be more powerfully leveraged and giving this feedback to others is a great way of showing respect, and. This approach uses your fresh perspective to great advantage.

No doubt you will have tremendous value to offer your organization by bringing ideas from your home country or former company, but it is often better to first show curiosity about your new company culture and Canadian approaches to work life. Your new co-workers will then be more comfortable in expressing their own curiosity about the unique perspectives you bring and ideas you can share from your cultural background and work history.

Be visible and approach others: Once you start in your new job, it may seem that the most important thing to do is to hunker down and get to work. However, it is equally, if not more, important that people meet you and get to know you as a colleague. You don't want to hide behind closed doors or in your cubicle. Be wary of eating lunch at your desk or away from others.

If others don't get to know who you are, they may make assumptions about you that are inaccurate. Canadian workplaces are generally relatively informal in that people expect to know at least a few details about one another's life outside of work. Bring in a few family photos or pictures that your children have drawn to personalize your work space and enable others to connect with you more readily.

Get clear about expectations: As soon as possible after you join a new organization, it is important to get clarity on:

- Expectations of you
- Expectations that you have of others (particularly your manager)

Clarifying expectations involves having a clear understanding of the mandate of the role, job description, objectives and performance measures. You may need to be proactive to obtain the specifics. The conversations between you and your manager or supervisor should involve agreeing upon desired outcomes and behaviours.

Some helpful questions for clarifying expectations are:

- What does your manager need you to do in the short term and in the medium term?
- What does success in your new role look like to your manager?
- What do you need to accomplish in the position that hasn't been done before?

• What are your internal customers and peers expecting of you?

If your new role is responsible for supervising others, it will be very helpful for them if you clarify your own expectations, describe your leadership style, preferred modes of communication and ways you'd like to be updated.

Be authentic: The pressure of meeting the expectations of a new role, new boss and new organization can lead some new hires to try so hard in their role that they end up "acting a part". This is particularly true for new immigrants who are often trying hard to "fit in" to the Canadian culture. This persona can be very difficult to maintain over time and can get in the way of developing strong relationships with others in your new environment.

Most Canadian organizations expect authenticity and integrity. Ironically, the research shows that in the Canadian culture, the leaders who are held in highest esteem are those who demonstrate the self-awareness and humility to let others know about areas of weakness or aspects of their role that they find challenging.

Some hiring managers equate "being yourself" with having good ethics. The reverse is also true. People that are seen as behaving in ways that are inconsistent with their values or who interact with one group of employees one way and another in a different way, may be seen as inauthentic and unethical in their behaviour.

Ask for help, establish support systems: When people join a new organization, typically they leave behind the established support systems that they have been relying on for help. When you are also immigrating to a new country, this challenge is compounded exponentially. Where you might have once felt very secure in knowing who you could trust and depend upon, now you may feel like you are essentially starting from scratch.

It is crucial to develop relationships with new work colleagues to provide insight into the real workings of the company, to help get things done efficiently, and to simply be a sounding board when the going gets tough.

People who effectively leverage resources around them and are proactive about seeking help are those who are best able to maximize their impact. In the Canadian work culture, asking for help is seen as a smart strategy, not a sign of weakness.

In addition to new work colleagues, many new hires rely heavily on trusted family members or life partners, particularly for emotional support during a stressful time. Others draw on the services of an external professional coach. Some people rely on journaling and self-reflection as a means of ensuring that they optimize their own learning during this challenging time.

Make early decisions on small, quick fixes: Some new hires put an inordinate amount of pressure on themselves to try to figure out "what's the most dramatic improvement I can make in my first three months, so that I can demonstrate my worth?" Yet, my research suggests that the best way to create early wins is to generate some relatively easy, quick fixes that provide relief for others and create tangible results. Look around for small issues that have frustrated others for some time, yet no one has gotten around to dealing with them.

Eliminating a barrier that is getting in the way of direct reports' accomplishments has a resounding impact. Making early decisions on small, quick fixes allow you to demonstrate good judgment, while minimizing risk.

By applying these tips and putting your best foot forward, I have no doubt that you will not only survive but THRIVE in your new role!

Sue Edwards is President of Development By Design, Leadership Coaching and Onboarding

Chapter 23

Keeping Your Job Once You Are On Board

By Arie Ball

> *"Every job is a self-portrait of the person who did it. Autograph your work with excellence."*
>
> ~ Unknown

Once you're onboard with a company, you need to:

1. understand the expectations of the job and your performance goals
2. be a team player
3. invest in yourself and your role.

At my company, we have a strong performance-based culture. As such, managers schedule annual meetings with their direct reports to discuss performance goals and expectations, as well as career growth and development. Our employees often engage in course-work, training, networking and mentoring to help themselves grow personally and professionally, which impact their job satisfaction and, in turn, overall employee retention.

As an employee, it's also extremely important for you to take the initiative to learn about what is expected of you over the coming year and to work towards those ambitions. This is where teamwork can be the key to your success.

How to Advance on the Job

Early in my career, I believed that career advancement was based solely on having a strong work ethic and solid performance results. While I still believe that there is no substitute for hard work and strong performance, what I learned over time is that being successful is also highly influenced through the learning that takes place and the exposure to new perspectives gained through mentoring relationships and building your networks.

To advance your career, you need to build in time to lift your head up from work, take a look around and connect with professionals inside your company and externally in your industry. You also need to be a continuous learner – whether through on-the-job training, volunteering for assignments or through prescribed coursework.

Arie Ball is Vice President of Sourcing and Talent Acquisition

Chapter 24

Ten Tips for Improving Your Work Life Without Leaving Your Job

---

By Maureen McCann

> *"The spirit, the will to win, and the will to excel are the things that endure. These qualities are so much more important than the events that occur."*
>
> ~Vince Lombardi,
> former American Football Player and Coach

Not everyone loves their job. And when people don't enjoy what they do, they tend to look around for problems that don't exist. If you're one of the unlucky people who don't like what you do, here are a few ideas to help you get through each day until you're ready to move on.

1. **Strengthen your boundaries:** Set firmer rules for yourself about your working hours, what you're willing to accept and what you will not. You'll want to ease into this slowly, making only minor adjustments to your schedule before sharing these changes with the people you work with/for. You don't need to be anyone's doormat.

2. **Look for the positives:** You may find that the job you are in is not exactly what you expected or it has changed over time to be something you do not enjoy. If this is so, try to find the positives

aspects of the job and work with those until you can make your move into a much better environment.

3. **Be realistic:** There are things at your place of employment you can change, and things you cannot. Have the wisdom to know the difference. You're probably not going to get the corner office if you've just started. At the same time, if you work hard, have a plan in place and give yourself time to do the work, you may get that corner office eventually.

4. **Take a break:** Schedule your vacation, take a long weekend or whatever you need to do to escape what is happening at the office. Take some time to gain perspective about your work situation. Having the time to reflect and plan will do your career all kinds of good. So go ahead, get out of there for a few days.

5. **Start doing more of what you love:** Identify and pursue things that interest you. These may be hobbies or volunteer work or something else altogether. The point is to bring "joy" into your life in a way that is not directly tied to your work life. Once you find something, continue to build on it, adding more joy as you find time. You're looking to re-ignite your sense of "intrinsic reward".

6. **Join groups:** Start small, then once you feel you're ready to take on more, set goals to meet new people, connect with others who share your interests. Maybe you'll join a professional association, a networking group or a speaking group. Perhaps there is an alumni group you've been meaning to reconnect with or a travel group that looks interesting. Whatever it is, take one step towards making it happen this week.

7. **Be receptive:** People bring their own unique perspective to a situation. Remember that your experience is yours and you are not to expect everyone to respond to circumstances the way

you would. There is more than one way to do things and yours may not be the way (this time). Accept this as a universal truth.

8. **Define a long-term strategy:** To get to where you want to be, you must first ***know*** where you want to be. A general or vague answer will not do (richer, more successful, promoted from here to there). You need to get much more specific: Within five years, I will be a professional writer with six e-books, three blogs and one New York Times best-seller, I will make $X/year, work 4 days a week, and vacation in the south of France.

9. **Use short-term goals as stepping stones:** Now that you specifically know what you want, you'll look for opportunities to pursue each of these. For example, you might start taking writing classes. You might begin researching areas in the south of France. You might uncover an opportunity to meet a well-established publisher who might offer to publish your book. (Don't hold your breath on this happening out-of the blue, by the way... You've got to work to make it happen).

10. **Identify companies:** Before you start Google-searching companies in your area, heed this warning: ONLY look for companies who are hiring people with the skills you most enjoy using. What's the sense in offering an employer skills you don't enjoy using? Yes, we can all clean a toilet. In fact, some of us are very good toilet cleaners; some of us even enjoy cleaning toilets, but it doesn't mean we want to make a career out of it.

Remember steps 8 and 9: Define a long-term strategy and use short-term goals as stepping stones. How is toilet cleaning going to get you closer to becoming a New York Times best-selling author? You're looking for ways to enhance those writing skills, learn more about southern France, get to know publishers and authors, so the companies you want to target should help you do that.

These steps aren't always easy to implement, nor are they a direct link to your dream job. They are, however, tips and strategies that may alleviate stress in your workplace and focus you in a more positive direction towards career success.

Maureen McCann is a Chief Career Strategist and Owner, ProMotion Career Solutions

Chapter 25

How to Get Noticed

> *"Believe in yourself and all that you are. Know that there is something inside you greater than any obstacle."*
>
> ~ Christian D. Larson,
> New Thought Leader & Teacher

It is quite possible you have been frustrated, watching others at your level move up the career ladder while you remain firmly rooted in your current position. Chances are you are working very hard but you are relying on others to take notice and offer you a promotion. You may have a long wait.

A project manager client went into the promotion conversation on the assumption that his director knew him very well. Unfortunately, that was not enough to give him the position he was after. Someone else was able to articulate their value and was promoted instead of the client.

Modesty has its place but if you don't learn to tell stories about yourself and take credit for your accomplishments, you will miss out on opportunities for promotion. Consider this situation: After being stuck in her position as an assistant manager in a bank for four years, one client said to me recently, "I am busy producing results. It's my manager's responsibility to promote me." This was after the manager told her she needed to start speaking up and letting others know about her achievements.

How often does one hear a manager encouraging a direct report to speak up and brag about their achievements? Not often. In fact, one's career trajectory is no longer the responsibility of a manager, the company's HR or training department. If you are looking for a promotion, it is your responsibility to take charge and guide your career. The following career-enhancing strategies should help you win a promotion.

Start Your Conversation With Facts and a Well-Thought-Out Plan

Any conversation about a promotion must begin with facts and a well-thought out plan. Don't assume everyone, including your manager, is aware of all that you do, so provide specifics about your successes.

Refer to the notes you have been keeping and the comments and testimonials you have received. When you are able to provide evidence of your accomplishments, it increases your chances for a promotion.

Use the "Vacuum Theory" as a Stepping Stone

The term *vacuum theory*, used in this context, has nothing to do with physics, but more to do with someone recognizing there is a job to be done and just doing it without being asked. You fill this vacuum by volunteering for the mundane tasks that no one else will do – work that is necessary but might not carry any prestige. Jump in, fill that vacuum and make a difference. Then, take the theory one step further and document what you have done. Your notes will become valuable in later conversations.

Ditch the Negative Self-Talk

Stop all the self-sabotaging conversations with yourself as these will stifle your chances of being promoted. Self-defeating, negative conversations such as, "Why should they promote me?" "They already have someone in mind, so why bother?" or "What's so special about me, anyway?" have no place in a promotion strategy. They keep you stuck. Focus your energies on your talents, abilities and contributions, and use them as leverage when discussing promotional opportunities with your manager.

Go the Extra Mile

Not only should you continue to be absolutely amazing in your current role, but you need to go the extra mile where it's never crowded. Your aim is to stand out. Become the "go-to" person – the one with the expertise that everyone turns to when they get stuck. Volunteer for assignments that are slightly outside your comfort zone – something that will stretch you but gives you an opportunity to learn new skills or demonstrate your expertise. When you take on additional tasks and projects, it proves you are who you say you are as well as who you want to be.

Develop a Marketing Strategy to Get Noticed

You need to become visible to influencers. These are individuals who will be able to attest to your abilities. Now, do not interpret this act as kowtowing or brown-nosing. It is a way to bring awareness of your existence and contributions. The reality is that if you don't toot your own horn, no one will know that you are coming.

How do you keep these influencers informed about your accomplishments? Identify projects you are working on and provide them with updates, especially if they have a connection to some of those projects. Share informative resources: audios, videos, books or links to articles that would be of interest to them. This not only shows your unselfish nature, but showcases the quality and level of your engagement.

Reesa Staten, Senior Vice President, Corporate Communications for Robert Half, said this about her mom: "My mom never missed an opportunity to ask for a raise or promotion when she felt she deserved one, and she didn't shy away from changing jobs when it meant more money or better benefits." Follow her advice.

The above strategies can help you tell your stories, stand out and get the promotion you deserve.

Chapter 26

Be Strategic in Advancing Your Career

By Lori-Anne Fitzpatrick

> *"Nothing in life just happens. You have to have the stamina to meet the obstacles to overcome them."*
>
> ~ Golda Meir, Former Israeli Prime Minister

While preparing for the interview for the role that I am currently in, I came up with the approach outlined below after thinking through some of the interviews that I had had with some past candidates and reviewing why I did not hire some of them who initially appeared to be strong. I prepared by identifying nine customers and two former employees of the team that I would manage if I was successful in the role.

I asked each contact a series of questions such as:

- How did they enjoy the experience that they received from the team?
- Were there any areas of improvement that they could see? Were there any changes that needed to be made immediately,
- Did they feel that the team had the rights skills to do the job?
- What challenges did they encounter when dealing with the team?

I then took the feedback from these contacts and created a three-month and one-year plan of what I would do differently if I were the successful candidate. When I went to the interview for the role I was asked what I knew about the team and I was able to craft an answer that gave some positive points and that highlighted some areas of opportunity.

I was asked how I would familiarize myself with the team culture. and I was able to speak to the research that I had done which I then turned into a question back to the interviewer regarding their view of the team.

I was asked what I would do in the role if I were the successful candidate and I then walked the interviewer through my three-month and my one-year plans.

What Made the Story Unique?

When I conduct interviews, I often ask questions about the industry or, if the candidate is internal, I ask questions about large initiatives funded by the company. The purpose is to gauge if the candidate is keeping up to speed with current events

What Did I Do Differently in My Interview?

When I interviewed for my current role, which was an internal posting, I prepared by identifying five large projects that the company was launching in the next 24 months. I obtained some high-level documents that described the projects and that outlined what the benefits of each would be.

I took a week's vacation prior to the final interview with the senior vice president (SVP) of the organization that I would be part of if I were the successful candidate. I read each project document and made brief notes regarding what the project was intended to do: what were the key financial benefits (i.e., would save $1million a year in operating costs), and what business initiatives each would support.

At the interview, the SVP asked me if I had heard of one of the projects. I was able to say in a few short sentences that I was aware of the project and that it would bring a number of benefits. I was also able to state what those benefits were.

When Hiring Candidates

In my current role, I hire people managers and technical managers. When hiring people managers, I look to the candidate to identify how many people they have managed; what level their staff were/are at (i.e., analyst, supervisor, etc.); what techniques the candidate uses to manage a team; what techniques they use to identify if the team is performing; examples of management actions (i.e., performance management, disciplinary actions, termination etc.), and examples of time management.

When hiring technical managers, I look for certifications (Bachelor of Computer Science, SQL certification, etc.); business process knowledge (flow charting, project plans, etc.); financial management experience; project management experience; information systems knowledge; client partnership; problem solving, and good communication.

Lori-Anne Fitzpatrick is the Director of Enterprise, Reporting & Analytics, Rogers Communications

Chapter 27

Sponsorship – Essential for Career Success

By Christine Brown-Quinn and Jacqueline Frost

> *"If you are interested in fast-tracking your career, in getting that next hot assignment or making more money, what you need is a sponsor."*
>
> ~ Sylvia Ann Hewlett, Author

Ask any successful business person whether there was anyone who really helped them to attain what they've achieved and they're bound to mention at least one person. This is the person who helped make things happen for them, especially in a corporate environment. Although the word "sponsor" might not have been used, this is fundamentally what a sponsor does.

Mentors vs Sponsors

Mentors, coaches, sponsors are all the same, right? Wrong. They are very different and serve very different purposes.

Over the last five years there has been a lot of talk about using mentors and coaches to develop high-potential professionals. Mentors and coaches are in effect advisors. They work behind the scenes and can be a powerful weapon to help you navigate challenging business environments. They can offer you valuable insights, act as a sounding board and even provide you with a shoulder to cry on. They are not, however, sponsors.

If you're interested in career progression, especially to the more senior levels, it's career sponsorship that's going to make that defining difference. Sponsors are very much out in the open. They are visible supporters and champions of your career. They are well-connected to the organization, and even industry, and have insider knowledge about opportunities (and threats!).

Formal vs Informal Sponsorship

Although an increasing number of companies are implementing *formal* sponsorship programs, especially for female professionals, there is no substitute for informal or organic sponsorships. The advantage of formal sponsorship is that the "matching" can happen quickly and it may be well supported by senior management. The disadvantage of these "arranged marriages" is that the connections aren't well tested as they haven't developed naturally. Therefore organic or informal sponsorships tend to be more sustainable and also not limited to one individual, division or department.

Like so many aspects of career development, things work best when you're in the driver's seat. You need to be clear about where you want to go and, with this bigger strategic picture or personal business plan in mind, think about who would make the best sponsor or sponsors.

How Do I Get a Sponsor?

Make no mistake about it, career sponsorship is not something that's given to you or that you can even ask for, but rather it has to be earned. And this is the case regardless of whether it's formal or informal. Ultimately, sponsors are interested in developing their protégés and they do this by connecting sponsorees to important players, projects and positions.

Given that sponsors are really going out on a limb for you, not only do you have to earn sponsorship, but you have to continue to be a stellar performer and show loyalty. It's an ongoing commitment rather than a one-off transaction. The downside is that if you don't hold up your end of the bargain, the sponsor will quickly pull their support in order to preserve their own reputation. As is the case in any company, bad news spreads fast so your reputation will be damaged as a result.

One of the most common questions we get asked by our clients is, "how do I earn sponsorship from someone who is more senior than I am?" It's about building a relationship and earning that trust.

Building a Long-lasting Relationship

As the more junior person, you may be thinking, "what do I have to offer?" Don't underestimate what you can bring to the relationship because you are more junior. You will know and hear about what's happening on the ground. Sharing this with a more senior person in a way that's strategic and linked to a current challenge can be very powerful. Given your position, you may also have more detailed knowledge on a specific issue. Senior management is relying on you to know the details – know your stuff. Again, the challenge is to think about how this detailed knowledge you have might relate to the bigger picture or current challenge that the sponsor is facing or is involved with. Then you can add tangible, direct value.

Remember that building any relationship is about investing in the long term which may mean many small effective steps rather than a big-bang approach. Your sponsor is bound to be busy. Think about what is the best time of the day or week to approach them. Do they prefer face-to-face, phone calls or emails? Spend time planning out your interactions, however short or small, to make them impactful. Be sure to make your opening lines intriguing and interesting. Avoid phrases such as "Do you have time…", "Sorry to bother you…." More useful one-liners include, "Here's a fantastic piece of news you might be interested in", or "Just want to give you a heads-up that such and such is happening".

Being respectful of the sponsor's time requires making the interactions as concise, punchy and relevant as possible. As the relationship develops, you also might think about adding a little bit of subtle humour and fun into the dialogue. Your sponsor will appreciate it and your career is likely to benefit from it as well.

Christine Brown-Quinn and Jacqueline Frost are co-founders and managing directors of the virtual Women in Business Superseries, focusing on career development.

Chapter 28

Exploring 'STEM' Careers

By Stephen Hinton

> *"Stepping stones take you across the river from where you perhaps are stuck to where you dream of being."*
>
> ~Author Unknown

If you read any top ten job lists or government labour statistics, you will see that Science, Technology, Engineering and Mathematics (STEM) jobs are among the fastest growing and well-paid jobs. But many of these high-level jobs are going unfilled, even during this soft economy with thousands of people out of work. Why? Job seekers feel these jobs are out of reach because many of them require four-year technical degrees.

I can tell you unequivocally that this belief is a hoax. A myth. There are many STEM-related jobs that do not require technical degrees. Some, in fact, only require a week of hands-on training or certification. Interested in knowing more? The story about my client "Bruce" is one instance that shatters some myths of how non-technical people can acquire well-paying STEM jobs.

The Story of Bruce

In 2008, Bruce (name changed to protect the real person) was a music sales executive in New York City who had worked at prestigious record labels and with some of the most famous musical artistes in history. But the advent of the internet and digital downloaded music forced Bruce and others like him to look for new careers.

Because he was over 40 and had a liberal arts degree, Bruce's choices were limited to sales and non-technical roles which offered lower salaries or required relocation. The New York job market was tough and getting tougher by the day because of the impending recession. Bruce was determined to find a new career that offered future growth potential and the chance to use cutting-edge technology. He researched and networked until he met a friend who introduced him to green buildings.

The green building industry with its facets of government regulations, real estate, construction, energy efficiency, recycled materials and computerized systems offered Bruce a tantalizing opportunity to enter a fast-growing market of cutting-edge products and services.

Adding to the excitement, the US government and many local and state governments were implementing building codes which called for more green technology in newly constructed buildings. Bruce started pursuing opportunities, but hit the education and experience "wall" which limited his ability to apply for the higher-paying positions.

Bruce found out through networking that he could take the exam for the LEED Green Associate certification after meeting some initial prerequisites. The LEED Green Associate (LEED GA) is a green building certification specifically developed for non-technical professionals to expand their knowledge of construction, materials and regulations surrounding energy efficient green buildings. This was the ticket.

When Bruce contacted me he was already studying for the LEED exam, but wanted a different perspective on how to pursue a job in the green buildings market. He had read my articles on green certifications and licenses and decided to seek my advice. After our initial conversation, we concluded that Bruce needed the certification to solidify his career transition. A few weeks after passing the LEED exam, Bruce landed a one-year intern assignment with a New York City government agency developing regulations for green buildings. After that, he was offered a position at a green building consulting firm advising construction professionals on LEED building certification requirements.

What We Can Learn from Bruce

Albert Einstein once said, "It's not that I'm so smart, it's just that I stay with problems longer". The biggest lesson we can learn from Bruce's story is about being *consistent and persistent.* Bruce consistently looked for opportunities through networking and research. He was persistent when he ran into obstacles. Bruce advises commercial building owners on the ways to make their new building projects "greener" and more energy efficient. His job is just as important to the building owner as the architects who design the building and the maintenance personnel who will repair all of the building's systems.

The beauty of his story is he does not have experience in construction, engineering, architecture or building maintenance, but he has put himself in a position to learn.

STEM Jobs Accessible to People Without Technical Degrees

Here are some examples of STEM jobs that do not require a four-year technical degree but may require experience and some form of advanced training:

- Building inspectors
- Engineering technicians
- Environmental technicians
- Geomatics technicians
- Industrial and technology real estate agents
- Pharmacy, laboratory and x-ray technicians
- Recycling managers and landfill gas plant operators
- Water treatment operators

It is my hope that more people will explore STEM-related fields as their next career move.

Stephen Hinton is President of Hinton Human Capital

Chapter 29

Managing Conflict in the Workplace

By Julie Smith

> *Now when issues arise at work or in personal relationships, for that matter, I know it is fundamental for me to look deeply and objectively at my own contribution to them before expecting others to change and improve.*
>
> ~ Kevin Sharer, former CEO of Amgen and now senior lecturer at Harvard Business School

What do you do when you "clash" with a co-worker, your boss or even worse – your interviewer? Everyone experiences conflict in a professional situation at some point in their career. The big question is: how can you handle these situations with grace and achieve the best possible outcome?

With over 20 years of corporate management experience, I have discovered a simple but powerful approach to managing conflict using the concepts of meditation.

Today, I teach meditation techniques to corporate professionals and show them how to apply the concepts of meditation to their lives.

3 Steps to Managing Conflict (Based on the Concepts of Meditation)

You have probably heard Einstein's quote: "We cannot solve our problems with the same level of thinking that created them." This process reflects this statement by helping you transform your "thinking" towards the problem rather than focusing on the problem itself.

1. Step one is about tuning-in to your mind and emotions to clearly understand your thought process and emotions when the conflict is occurring. Many people are surprised at how unaware they are of their own thoughts and emotions!

2. Step two involves developing a kinder and more compassionate attitude towards the person you are in conflict with, which is often overlooked but key to improving relationships.

3. Step three helps you accept your emotions and come back to your centre point. In short, it helps you be at your best so you can respond in the best manner.

There are specific meditations and visualisations that can be used at each stage to help you deal with the conflict situation with more grace and ease. By using this powerful process, my clients and I have experienced a complete transformation in professional relationships – and I know it can work for you too!

Julie Smith is Founder of the Success Through Stillness Approach and Peaceful Sleep System

Chapter 30

Writing Your Story Can Help You Bounce Back

By Maureen McCann

"Success is how high you bounce when you hit bottom."
~ General George S. Patton,
US Army General

I loved the work I was doing. Loved it! The environment, however, was unbearable! I was working in a toxic workplace in which my employer was a bad leader and a bully. The staff morale was incredibly low. At the worst point, I found myself standing on the steps of the medical clinic convinced I was having a heart attack. It turned out it was a panic attack, but it scared me enough to take action and get myself out of an awful situation.

Bouncing Back to Leap Forward

So what can you do if you find yourself in a similar situation? Here are some approaches you can take to help you bounce back:

1. **Look for ways to bring joy to your life:** Sunday was the best day of the week. I would get up early, drive to the ski hill and teach children how to ski. It brought me so much joy I was bursting at the seams. This helped me regain the self-confidence I would need to move forward.

2. **Remove your limiting beliefs:** Many of us were taught "never leave a job until you have a job". Though it was incredibly painful, I summoned the courage to break this "rule". My mental health and well-being were worth more than the bi-weekly pay cheque I was earning.
3. **Seek counsel:** Don't keep your feelings to yourself. Find a trusted friend or professional with whom you can share your concerns or frustrations.
4. **Take actionable steps:** Thinking and planning will only get you so far. You must find the strength to make difficult decisions and put them into action. Will Rogers once said: "Even if you're on the right track, you'll get run over if you just sit there."
5. **Create a "love me" file:** Self-confidence is a terrible thing to lose. So create a file where you collect all the amazing things in your life. Mine contains heart-warming notes from friends, family, clients and colleagues. It boosts my spirits immensely and reminds me how my life has helped others. Working in a toxic workplace – those were dark days that saw me doubting my own potential. Fortunately, taking these steps has led me to a wonderfully fulfilling life both personally and professionally.
6. **Failure is in all of us:** "I've missed more than 9,000 shots in my career. I've lost almost 300 games. Twenty-six times, I've been trusted to take the game winning shot and missed. I've failed over and over and over again in my life. And that is why I succeed." ~ Michael Jordan
7. **Organize your thoughts:** Separate what is yours and take ownership of what you can change. Leave the rest behind. Organize your thoughts. Analyse how you failed on your part. Own the problem.

Maureen McCann is Chief Career Strategist and Owner, ProMotion Career Solutions

Chapter 31

Conquer Your Fears to Tell Your Story

> *"FEAR has two meanings: Forget Everything And Run, or Face Everything And Rise! The choice is yours!"*
>
> ~ Anonymous

American author Napoleon Hill said, "Every adversity, every failure, every heartache carries with it the seed of an equal or greater benefit." Nowhere is this more applicable than the rejection Brian Acton, co-founder of Whatsapp, received from both Twitter and *Facebook*. These days, Brian is laughing all the way to the bank, because *Facebook*, the company that once rejected him, purchased Whatsapp for $16 billion.

Many of us have faced rejection of some sort or another at some point in our lives. Sometimes it's a job offer that went to someone else; a promotion that didn't materialize or a response to an email rebuffing your LinkedIn invitation. The reality is that whatever the rejection, its initial impact is never pleasant. Because most of us tend to wrap our self-worth around our careers, when we are rejected, we tell ourselves that we don't have what it takes to succeed.

I remember how devastated I felt years ago when I lost out on a job that I thought had my name written all over it. After I got the bad news, I held a pity party the entire afternoon. I was the only one in attendance, and didn't I spend the time beating up and second-guessing myself?

I soon faced the reality that wallowing in self-pity wasn't going to help me. I brushed myself off, took an introspective look, and decided that I had too much to offer to spend time moaning and groaning over a lost opportunity. That self-assessment was the first step that helped to change the trajectory of my career and my life.

In my book, **No Canadian Experience, Eh?** I mentioned that the more "Noes" someone gets, the closer that person is to "Yes", and one "Yes" is all that's needed. As a job seeker, you may have received your quota of rejections, but this is not the time to give up. It's time to redouble your efforts. Count your "Noes" as stepping stones to "Yes"! Here are three tips to help you deal with a job rejection:

1. **Assess yourself.** Review the situation to see what went well and look for opportunities where you need to grow.
2. **Be courteous.** Notice that Brian Acton's tweet paid a compliment to the people he met at *Facebook*. He didn't engage in any bad- mouthing.
3. **Follow up with your interviewer.** Sometimes the candidate they chose didn't work out, but because of your professionalism and lack of bitterness, they could decide to offer you the position, or at least give you a second opportunity.

Just in case you believe you will never rise from the ashes of a rejection, below are some individuals who faced rejection in their lives, but went on to achieve great things:

- **Oprah Winfrey** was told she wasn't fit for television.
- **Jack Canfield** and **Mark Victor Hansen** received 144 rejections from publishers for their book **Chicken Soup for the Soul.**
- **Jay-Z** had big dreams to become a rapper, but couldn't get signed to any record labels. He created his own music empire: *Roc-A-Fella Records.*

- **J.K. Rowlings** got fired because she spent her time writing stories on her work computer.
- **Michael Jordan** was cut from his high school basketball team. He went home, locked himself in his room and cried.

While your story might not be as well-documented as these celebrities; while you might not aspire to such heights, you could change the direction of your life if you view rejection as an opportunity to start over. Bob Marley, in one of his songs, says, "As one door closes, another one opens." Don't continue staring at the closed door and miss other doors of opportunity.

You must realize that a few failures do not mean the end of your career journey. If you allow fear to get in your way, you will not be able to tell your story effectively to get hired. You have to believe in yourself and your abilities. You have to own your successes, then articulate them clearly and convincingly before employers will take you seriously. Here are some quotes about failure that should motivate you to keep trying:

- *"You gain strength, courage and confidence by every experience in which you really stop to look fear in the face. You must do the thing you think you cannot do."* ~ Eleanor Roosevelt, Former US First Lady

- *"Courage faces fear and thereby masters it."* ~ Martin Luther King Jr, American Pastor, Activist, Humanitarian

- *"In order to succeed, your desire for success should be greater than your fear of failure."* ~ Bill Cosby, American Comedian and Actor

- *"Nothing in life is to be feared. It is only to be understood."* ~ Marie Curie, Polish Physicist and Chemist

- *"There is only one thing that makes a dream impossible to achieve: the fear of failure."* ~ Paulo Coelho, Brazilian Lyricist and Novelist

- *"I learned that courage was not the absence of fear, but the triumph over it. The brave man is not he who does not feel afraid, but he who conquers that fear."* ~ Nelson Mandela, Former President of South Africa and Anti-apartheid Revolutionary

- *"Face your fears and doubts, and new worlds will open to you."* ~ Robert Kiyosaki, American Author and Investor

- *"Too many of us are not living our dreams because we are living our fears."* ~ Les Brown, Motivational Speaker and Author

- *"Failure is not failing to reach your goal...it is not having a goal. Failure is not failing to hit your target. . .it is not having a target. Failure is not falling down...it is refusing to get back up. Failure is not trying and not accomplishing anything....it failing to try. You're never a failure until you quit."* ~ Pastor Rick Warren, Saddleback Church, USA

Chapter 32

Developing an Exit Strategy

"We all take different paths in life, but no matter where we go, we take a little of each other everywhere."
~ Tim McGraw, American Singer and Actor

How to Leave a Job in Style

A few days before leaving the last company I worked with, I sent the following email to all 700 staff members:

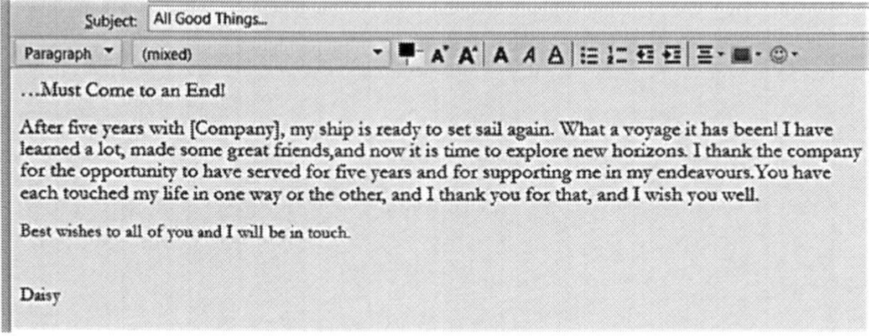

Subject: All Good Things...

Paragraph (mixed)

...Must Come to an End!

After five years with [Company], my ship is ready to set sail again. What a voyage it has been! I have learned a lot, made some great friends,and now it is time to explore new horizons. I thank the company for the opportunity to have served for five years and for supporting me in my endeavours.You have each touched my life in one way or the other, and I thank you for that, and I wish you well.

Best wishes to all of you and I will be in touch.

Daisy

This was not my resignation letter, but one person commented that it was the "nicest resignation letter" she had ever read. In retrospect, I didn't have to send it to everyone in the company, although indirectly I had connections to the entire staff .

Having said that, your departure does not have to be as thespian as mine. Neither does it have to be "sweet" as Chris Holmes's. Holmes is a former Border Agency official at London's Stansted Airport who left to pursue his dream as a chef. He wrote his resignation letter on a cake. While your exit from your company does not have to be dramatic, there are ways to leave with class.

The first rule of thumb is not to burn your bridges. Michelle Tillis Lederman, author of **The 11 Laws of Likability**, says, "Now is not the time to say all the things that you have built up. You never know when your paths will cross again." That is correct. Now is not the time to wash your dirty linen in public. You want to leave a lasting positive impression on your peers, your supervisor and the company.

Do you have unfinished work that could be completed before you leave? Set aside time to accomplish that task. Create a handy "how-to" manual that explains some of the nuts and bolts of the job. This will make it easy for your successor. In addition, offer to be available for a few weeks after you leave, if it is possible to do so. These small gestures will leave a lasting impact long after you are gone.

When I was leaving one other company, instead of leaving at the end of my two-week notice, I offered to spend the last three weeks training my replacement. Good karma paid off because the woman who I replaced at my new company made herself available to me for months after she left.

The Exit Interview

Most employers will hold an exit interview to find out why you made the decision to leave the company. Use the opportunity to give constructive ways they could improve employee morale, if that was an issue, or make suggestions on how they retain good employees. Your efforts will benefit the people you are leaving behind, and more important, demonstrate that you are still the professional they hired on day one.

Below is a list of questions that some employers ask during exit interviews. Review them so you will be prepared:

- What prompted you to resign?
- What did your new employer offer you that we didn't?
- What was the best part of working with us? What was the least?
- What did you like most about your job? What did you like least?
- What advice would you offer your supervisor or the company if you knew it would improve relations with our employees?
- How would you rate our compensation package against your new employer's?
- Would you consider working with us again?

SECTION IV

UNCONVENTIONAL WAYS TO TELL STORIES

"I've never liked categories; I've never liked boxes; I've always tried to be unconventional as much as I possibly could."

~Gary Dourdan, Actor

Chapter 33

Get Creative to Get Hired

"You begin by always expecting good things to happen."
~ Tom Hopkins, Master Sales Trainer

While success is not guaranteed, some job seekers have tried some innovative ways to tell their stories and get hired. Some may not have been hired, but they certainly got noticed. And, before you start saying those strategies won't work for you, because you are "not those people", think again. What out-of-the-box techniques can you think of that would get the attention of the one hiring manager or decision-maker you desperately want to meet?

Your techniques don't have to be as unconventional as the following examples, but when these individuals needed to separate themselves from the throng, they found creative ways to get attention, tell their stories and get hired. Even those who did not get hired, ended up hiring themselves.

Think of this woman who, it is alleged, used a "foot-in-the-door'" strategy to land her job. She wanted to work for the biggest advertising agency in town. She sent the owner a box with a shoe (a new one) along with a note that said, "Now that I have my foot in your door, I'd like to talk to you about a job."

"Outrageous," you say. "That would never work for me or anyone I know." It might or might not, but this lady had done her homework and knew this gentleman was likely to be impressed with her strategy. (She got the interview, and the job.) Bear in mind that companies hire when they see someone with the skillset they need...that's why you should aim to get your foot in the door long before the position is advertised.

Philip Dubost

Philip Dubost, a web product manager from Paris, was looking for a position where he could travel. He decided to create a unique résumé that would make him stand out anywhere in the world, so he created a résumé that looked exactly like an Amazon product page.

He took the initiative and spent the time to replicate every aspect of an Amazon page, inserting ads, and even stating that "Only 1 left, Order soon". How much more creative could one get?

Jenn Harris

Jenn Harris, CEO of High Heel Golfer, used the golfing skills she learned from her father to teach women how to play the game. Although this has become her new career, it was not in the forefront of her mind when she graduated from college.

She was working with a defence contractor and heard that a golf tournament was scheduled for clients. "Honestly, I wanted to play in the tournament but my boss said I wouldn't be able to communicate with the admirals. I think my boss not wanting me to play was more about age discrimination. However, he suggested that if I wanted to play, I could pay for it myself and take a vacation day. I opted out of playing like most women do.

"I was lucky that a client found out that I wanted to play and I was asked to play on our own time a few weeks later. We hit it off and it was shortly after, I was asked to be on all of the big projects. I got a promotion, along with job security, within nine months. However, budget cuts started rolling around, and the thought of starting my own business became a reality."

When asked how the client discovered that she could play golf, Jenn said, "The guys down at the branch knew I played golf because I told them. They also knew I had a big interest in playing in the golf tournament. My dad taught me that golf could help me connect with clients or colleagues in business, so I definitely let everyone know!

"It wasn't just the fact that I played golf that brought me the success, but the round of golf helped the clients see that I had drive and wanted to succeed and that I had the brains to do it. Without golf I would have been stuck in the cubicle working on basic tasks, golf helped me connect with people – something I love and do well."

Jenn quit her job and started her own female-focused golf business, specializing in teaching women golf etiquette – how to network on the golf course and build relationships.

In rounding out the conversation, Jenn said, "Golf is a place that levels the playing field for everyone, no matter what your age, specialty or gender." Rather than sit on the sidelines and watch, Jenn Harris turned an obstacle into an opportunity and created a career serving a niche for professional women.

Lauren Holliday

Lauren, a journalist and contributor to career website, **The Muse**, was quite focused on building her experience portfolio through unpaid internships. However, at age 20, her father thought she had done enough "free work", and said it was time to get a job that paid!

Like most job seekers do, Lauren submitted her résumé online for numerous positions that she was, and was not, qualified for. And, as is the norm with mass applications, she did not receive one phone call or email, except the automatic acknowledgement that her résumé was received.

She continued her job search, and finally landed one interview. She did not land that particular job, but it opened up a whole new world for her. It was during this interview that she was introduced to Constant Contact, an email marketing service. Somehow, she thought it could be used as a job search tool, and as soon as she arrived home, she took advantage of the one-week free trial that the company offered and decided to make the tool her new best friend.

It appeared to her that there was a better way to conduct a successful job search campaign rather than becoming lost in the résumé black hole.

"As a young professional in a competitive field, I needed to find a way to stand out to hiring managers. I needed to showcase my marketable skills and to present those skills in a unique and compelling way, but I also needed people to take a chance on me. And I needed to uniquely apply to a vast number of jobs in an extremely short amount of time," said Lauren.

While she was introduced to Constant Contact first, she later learned of MailChimp, another free email service, (unless a mailing list exceeded 2,000). (By the way, this is the same email service provider that I use to send my *CareerTips2Go* newsletters to clients.) Lauren then created an email marketing campaign. The result was that she was invited to 15 job interviews after investing only 30 minutes of her time. Within days, she had gone from unpaid intern to paid marketing director.

Here is a list of steps that Lauren took to land interviews and a job.

- Registered for a free account on MailChimp, and built a list of people who could potentially hire her. This included reviewing job postings to scrape the email addresses of hiring managers, or conducting further research to find email addresses.
- Developed an email campaign using MailChimp's easy-to-use, step-by-step process.
- Used an eye-catching Subject Line to capture the hiring manager's attention.
- Created an image (although not a graphic artist), consisting of her personal logo, and slogan "All I want to do is change the world."
- Used a "Try Before You Buy" approach to grab the attention of hiring managers and keep them engaged throughout her email. This is where her call-to-action was located, and where she explained exactly what she had to offer.
- Included three of her best portfolio samples that showed employers exactly what she could offer them; provided a link to her résumé, and her contact information, including social media profiles.
- Scheduled the time of delivery of her marketing campaign to ensure it was the first thing recipients saw when they opened their email the following day.

Her efforts resulted in 15 interview offers soon after sending the email, and within days she was hired.

Several hiring managers commented on her approach to her job search. They told her they loved her creativity, originality, and initiative. Lauren said, "They especially loved the "Try Before You Buy" tactic, as it made them laugh, made them like me and, as you know, being likable plays a huge part in a successful job search."

Michael Mahle

Michael Mahle is a communications professional who was looking for a job in the hospitality industry. He used Pinterest to create his résumé. In the centre of the résumé is a wine glass. Several strategies caught my attention on Michael's Pinterest résumé.

First, he stated exactly what he was looking for. "I'm looking for a high-level communications position (PR, marketing, advertising, etc.) in the wine world."

Second, instead of the usual "References Available on Request", he had a "Who I Know" section with the names of three references. This is not the norm on a traditional résumé. One would assume that the individuals he listed were influencers in his industry.

Third, the fact that he made his job search campaign quite visible online, it received the attention of people who either offered to help him or put him in touch with others who could help him.

One man wrote, "Would you be interested in Marriott or Hilton World HQ in DC Metro area? I have many contacts at each – send me an invite to connect on LI [LinkedIn] and I will accept. Great work! Very targeted and persuasive!"

Marguerite Orane

"I arrived in Toronto in August 2009 ready to conquer the world. Life was good in Jamaica but it was going to be even better in Canada! Did I have a plan for when I arrived? I guess I did – but you know what they say: 'Life is what happens when you are busy making other plans.'

“About eight months into my settling in, doing ad hoc projects and teaching at Ryerson, my resources were starting to dwindle. Uh oh, this wasn’t what is supposed to happen. I was supposed to get rich, not poor. After one too many times of hearing ‘we don’t have the money’ my daughter Victoria yelled: ‘Then why don’t you get a job.’

“Huh? A job? I haven’t had one of those since 1990, having been happily self-employed since then. But this is Canada, and I needed to be open to new things. So off I went on a job hunt odyssey. I quickly learned that looking for a job is a full-time job, and there is a long learning curve.

“This hunt took six months of digging deeper into my savings. As an independent woman all my life, I did not like it. Over the ensuing months, despair set in. I came to Canada armed with a Harvard MBA, certification as a coach and facilitator, numerous years in consulting, including for the Canadian government and Canadian consulting firms and 10 years actually running businesses. WOW! Even I was impressed when I looked at my résumé.

“Yet it didn’t seem to mean anything to the “File 13” hole that I swear my applications fell into. I did everything “they” said to do:

- I reworked and revised my résumé to death
- I networked incessantly
- I applied online, crafting my cover letters for the nuances of each job
- I pulled whatever strings I had in Canada.

“No job. I did get a few interviews but those led nowhere. Friends and acquaintances gave advice such as: ‘Take Harvard off your résumé’; ‘Don’t put your age’; ‘Replace 30 years experience with 15-plus years’ and so on. I started to doubt myself and all that I had achieved for it seemed to mean nothing in Canada. And I sunk really low when I found myself asking questions such as: Was it because I was black, a woman, have an accent?

"On October 27, 2010, everything changed. I was in an interview at one of the big banks. I was sitting in front of this woman, telling her about a time when, all of a sudden, I saw myself as if outside of my body. And I realized that I did not want this job; I did not want to work for this woman, and I did not want to work for this organization. Yet, if the job was offered to me I would have taken it. I was that desperate.

"And something snapped. Within the 45-minute subway ride home I had decided I am done with asking and begging people for a job: I was going to do what I have always done – make my own job. And so, right there on the TTC I abandoned my job search and decided to start (or may I say re-start) my own consulting and leadership business.

"As I look back, I reflect on at least three lessons:

1. **Stay true to who you are**. This allows you to get very clear on what you want. When you are clear, the whole universe will conspire to give it to you. Once I reminded myself of who Marguerite is, and made the decision to start my own business, within 24 hours I got an e-mail from a client asking me to come to Jamaica in January to do a retreat!

2. **NO is sometimes a better answer than YES**. I am now so grateful for the people who told me 'no'; all the people who didn't even have the courtesy to reply to my applications. The man in charge of leadership development for a big bank who virtually laughed me out of his office. The people who were kind enough to say 'you're great, but not what we need right now'. NO closes doors and opens space for a bigger YES!

3. **Don't worry.** One thing that kept me going through the down days was my daily walks with my dogs. I would leash them up and we would head out to the park, no matter how unhappy I was feeling. And as I walked them, I would sing my favourite Bob Marley song: "*Don't worry 'bout a thing, cause every little thing gonna be all right.*" And it is.

Hanna Phan

Hanna Phan lost her job as an IT (information technology) engineer a few years ago. Because of the tough economic market and so many people vying for so few positions, she decided not to use the traditional résumé for her job search.

After much research, she found her ideal company, SlideRocket, a company that makes presentation software products. Instead of sending a traditional résumé, Phan used the company's own product to create her presentation résumé. She then created a social media campaign to market herself. One of the first things she did was to tweet the following message to the then CEO of Sliderocket, Chuck Dietrich:

"@chuckdietrich @sliderocket: I want to work with you! Find my application here:
http://portal.sliderocket.com/AIWCI/Iwanttoworkatsliderocket"

Within an hour, and fresh off the plane, the CEO responded:
"@hannaphan @sliderocket AMAZING Preso! Let's talk."

Prior to its acquisition by ClearSlide, SlideRocket was a part of the VMWare Family, where Phan currently works.

Sukhjit Singh

"Like the majority of internationally-educated professionals moving to Canada, I faced many employment barriers when I arrived. First, I didn't have 'Canadian experience', to get a job. Second, no one offered me a job so I could get the Canadian experience they required. Third, I was told by many people that no one would hire me because, as a Sikh, I wear a turban and a beard.

"Considering that I had a Masters of Business Administration, specializing in IT, and a Bachelor of Science in Computer Engineering, I was very disappointed to hear all these negative conversations, but I was not deterred. I decided I would use such negative perceptions to spur me forward.

"As a newcomer, I had heard of several integration and employment workshops offered by various non-profit organizations. During one of these workshops I found the website for Volunteer MBC and saw that the local YMCA was looking for a volunteer to teach computer courses.

"I jumped at the opportunity and began facilitating courses at the beginner, intermediate and advance levels. I was enjoying it so much that I took my volunteering efforts to other organizations. This turned out to be a win-win, as I was meeting new people, and learning a lot about Canadian culture, while imparting my expertise to others.

"Many people frown when they hear about volunteering. Some worry that it won't pay the bills; others view it negatively because of the experiences they have had. Some believe that because they are not being paid, it is useless work. I included my volunteer experience on my résumé and that helped me to secure paid positions. In fact, I believe that my volunteer experience has been the greatest contributor to my success in Canada. Not only was I able to learn new skills, and find paid and volunteer positions, but these skills helped me to serve in various roles such as settlement worker, enhanced language training coordinator, information counsellor and interpreter/translator.

"In three short years, and as a result of my volunteerism, I moved from being unemployed to becoming one of the Top 25 Canadian Immigrants. I am also the recipient of the Newcomer Volunteer Gem Award from Volunteer MBC, a local volunteer organization.

"As I have said many times, volunteer work is like getting a university degree in networking and Canadian culture for free – except those degrees would be hard to come by, so the value is even greater.

"My experiences demonstrate the positive aspects of volunteering. You, too, will be able to meet great people, learn new skills, and advance your career."

Razwana Wahid

"Dreams start with What if…?, Living starts with Why Not…?".

"I was drawn to the bright lights of London. The home town where I grew up served me well for the time I spent there. I managed to navigate through different jobs. (I couldn't survive working in a company for more than 18 months!), but then things just stagnated. I saw people around me working for the same circle of companies and eventually retiring. The thought of that being my life made me want to stick a needle in my eye.

"So London seemed like an exciting place to go: new people, new place, and new opportunities. So I packed my bags and left. Very early into my first job in London, I realized that neither the job nor the boss were what I had signed on for. In fact, it was the moment the owner of the company decided not to pay us!

"I hadn't done my due diligence on this company and had thought that since he was a referral from a friend, I could trust him. Turned out my friend had no idea of the financial trouble the company was in. My employer was certainly convincing and talked a good game.

"But I had spent my life savings to move to London. Not being paid was the worst thing that could've happened to me at the time. So I left that job in search of another and that took another four months and thousands of dollars in debt to finally get there. It was one of the lowest points of my life.

"I knew I needed a transformation. There were many factors, other than the loss of a job, that lead me to that situation – none of which I would change for a second. The entire experience taught me resilience, persistence and made me realise that even though there is opportunity in adversity, going back to basics is sometimes necessary.

"So I got another job and stuck it out until my debt was paid off, then took another when that contract ended. That second job was what introduced me to a new client and I moved to Paris with a new employer. After I caught my breath, I decided it was time to listen to my instincts and start my own business. I hadn't spent more than 18 months in a job after all, so I figured that these short stints had to mean something!

"My story is not just about job losses, debt and rising from those perceived failures. It's about looking back at patterns in my life and seeing them for what they were. It's about exploring my values and really understanding what it is that makes me feel alive. For me, I value freedom, connection and courage. Those three things are paramount in my life. The freedom to choose. Connections with people.

And taking bold, courageous action. Without any of those things, I would never have moved to London, and perhaps would never have ended up where I am today.

"So people who are deciding on their next move shouldn't try and 'find their passion'. Instead, take time to know who you are. Your values and beliefs about life will drive you towards that next step."

Guillermo Ziegler

"I am one of those internationally-educated professionals who arrived in Canada with a big dream. My previous experiences included being a programmer, system administrator, teacher, technical salesman, software tester, among others.

"That blend of experiences served both as my weakness and my strength. I was an experienced professional with a proven record in many different fields, but not considered an expert in one particular technology. With such a diverse background, I was still able to tell my story and was selected by one of the world's most influential companies in Canada. I started working on a new project at their offices in Southwestern Ontario.

"During my almost eight years with the company, I witnessed the many ups and downs of this technology giant. I had the chance to experiment with some of the latest technologies in a field that was rapidly growing and where competition was getting fierce at a very fast pace. The struggles of the company, brought on by the competition, led to layoffs, and I was among one of the many individuals affected by this.

"At this point in my career I had to do some self-searching. What does someone do when he has worked for more than seven years for the same company, doing almost the same job day by day, feeling warm and safe in his chair? What is he going to do with all that free time? And even more, how is he going to deal with a job market that is asking for skills that he may probably not have after seven years? This is what I did: I used a tripod approach, and a 'BAG'.

"That 'tripod' was my **Network, Job Boards** and **LinkedIn**.

Network: I tried to reach as many people as possible and make them aware of my situation. I was very pragmatic; to be unemployed is not a shame, especially because it was initiated by the company and not through any fault of mine. I reached out, asked for a coffee and in that coffee shop asked my contacts this one question: "What would you do if you were in my shoes?" Some of the answers I received were surprising, but I learned lots of things by asking. I was also able to reach out to other people, resulting in interviews in several instances.

Job Boards: While job boards are important – they gave me an idea of which companies were hiring, and what skills they were looking for – they complement the other two parts of the 'tripod'. With job boards and job alerts, you may be bombarded with many job opportunities. Make sure to analyse each position to separate what is worthy and what is not, then apply only to those that you feel would be a good fit. Also, use *LinkedIn* to check if your network has a tie to that company or to a hiring manager. You want to ensure your résumé goes directly to someone who can put in a word for you, or goes straight to the decision maker.

LinkedIn: Since I knew recruiters are always out there 'in the cloud' looking for people like me, I did a number of things. I made sure I had a very good profile. I reviewed the contacts in my network, but also went on a mission to reach out to potential contacts. This exercise helped me to make new contacts and ask past colleagues for references.

"While networking, make sure your conversation covers the 'BAG' areas: Your **B**ackground, **A**ccomplishments and **G**oals. The BAG is a perfect way to answer three key questions: Who are you? What do you have to offer? What problems have you solved? These three key questions helped me, not only to network, but to keep me focussed on the stories I wanted to tell in order to be hired.

My overall strategy worked extremely well for me. After 50 days of job search (including statutory holidays), I was offered a one-year contract with another high profile software company.

Links

Section I – Telling Your Story

This section contains a list of links that were referenced in the book:

The Clues to a Great Story
http://www.ted.com/talks/andrew_stanton_the_clues_to_a_great_story.html

The Art of Storytelling for Remarkable Leaders
http://www.youtern.com/thesavvyintern/index.php/2012/04/11/the-art-of-storytelling-for-remarkable-leaders/

Losing the Plot
http://careersintheory.wordpress.com/2012/03/14/losing-the-plot/

The Benefits of Storytelling to Children
http://youtu.be/goclMA_-fvs

What's Your Story? Tell it And you May Win a Prize
http://www.nytimes.com/2012/04/22/business/russell-goldsmith-of-city-national-on-storytellings-power.html?_r=2&ref=jobs

The Science of Storytelling
http://www.pbs.org/newshour/rundown/2012/06/on-the-science-of-storytelling.html

The Connect Effect – Networking Quotient (NQ)
http://www.theconnecteffect.com/?page_id=3

Networking for Results
http://www.michaeljhughes.com/dna/dna.php

Michael J Hughes – the Ottawa Networking Guru
http://www.michaeljhughes.com/about.php

Donna Fisher – a Premier Networker
http://www.donnafisher.com/whoisdonnafisher.html

Networking Today
http://www.networkingtoday.com/networking-group-details/ON/Ottawa/Fuchsia%20Factory%20Speed%20Networking-250

Career Management Site
www.jibberjobber.com

Your Body Language Shapes Who You Are
http://www.ted.com/talks/amy_cuddy_your_body_language_shapes_who_you_are

Section II – Job Search Strategies

How My Personal Website Helped Me Land My Dream Job
https://www.themuse.com/advice/how-my-personal-website-helped-me-land-my-dream-job

15 Rules for Negotiating a Job Offer
http://hbr.org/2014/04/15-rules-for-negotiating-a-job-offer/

6 Strategies to Get a Raise Without Asking
http://www.glassdoor.com/blog/6-strategies-raise/

How to Tell Your Professional Story on LinkedIn
http://www.inc.com/steve-cody/how-to-tell-your-professional-story-on-linkedin.html

Insider Tips From an Expert MBA Recruiter*
http://poetsandquants.com/2014/04/03/insider-tips-from-an-expert-mba-recruiter/
*All references to Sandy Khan were derived from this article

Job Proposal Letter
http://job.1-page.com/en-US/pages/how-it-works

Section IV – Unconventional Ways To Tell Stories

Philippe Dubost
http://www.phildub.com/

Lauren Holliday
https://www.themuse.com/advice/how-i-landed-15-job-interviews-in-30-minutes

How a SlideRocket Employee Landed Her Dream Job
https://blogs.vmware.com/careers/2011/10/how-a-sliderocket-employee-landed-her-dream-job.html

Michael Mahle
Michael Mahle on Pinterest

Create Your Own Career: How 6 Women Did It
http://www.dailyworth.com/posts/2521-these-women-created-their-own-unconventional-career-paths/

Reading Resource List

The following is a list of books that were used during the research and writing process. Even if direct quotes were not used from these books, at some point they provided inspiration and motivation when the going got tough. By listing them here, I am paying tribute to the authors.

- *Boost Your Interview IQ*, Carole Martin
- *Ditch, Dare, Do: 66 Ways to Become Influential, Indispensable, and Incredibly Happy at Work*, William Arruda & Deb Deb
- *Forget a Mentor, Find a Sponsor: The New Way to Fast Track Your Career*, Sylvia Ann Haylett
- *Left to Tell: Discovering God Amidst the Rwandan Holocaust*, Immaculee Ilibagiza
- *No Canadian Experience, Eh? A Career Success Guide for New Immigrants*, Daisy Wright
- *Negotiating Your Salary: How to Make $1,00 a Minute*, Jack Chapman
- *Self-Promotion for Introverts: The Quiet Guide to Getting Ahead*, Nancy Ancowitz
- *Significant! From Frustrated to Franne-tastic: Inspirational stories for the entrepreneurial woman*, Franne McNeal
- *Step Aside Super Woman: Career & Family is for Any Woman*, Christine Brown-Quinn
- *Tell to Win: Connect, Persuade, and Triumph with the Hidden Power of Story*, Peter Guber
- *The Bible*

- *The Canadian Career Strategist* (ebook Study Guide), 4th edition, *Sharon Graham*
- *The Daniel Plan Series,* Rick Warren
- *The Emperor Has No Clothes: Conquering Self-Doubt to Embrace Success,* Joyce M. Roché
- *The MomShift: Women Share Their Stories of Career Success After Having Children,* Reva Seth
- *Why Not You? 28 Days to Authentic Confidence,* Valorie Burton
- *Your Network is Your Net Worth: Unlock the Power of Connections for Wealth, Success, and Happiness in the Digital Age,* Porter Gayle

List of Contributors

Arie Ball
Vice President Talent Acquisition, Sodexo
Website: www.sodexoUSA.com
Careers Blog: sodexousacareersblog.com
Email: Arie.Ball@Sodexo.com

Audrey Prenzel
Résumé Resources Inc.
Website: www.resumeresources.ca
Email: resumeresources@gmail.com

Carole Martin
President, The Interview Coach
Website: www.interviewcoach.com

Christine Brown-Quinn & Jacqueline Frost
Women in Business Superseries
Website: www.womeninbusinesssuperseries.com/
Email: info@wibconsulting.com

Guillermo Ziegler
Ziegler Immigration Coaching
Website: www.ziglerimmigrationcoaching.com
guillermo@ziegleric.com

Jenn Harris
CEO, High Heel Golfer
Email: jenn@highheelgolfer.com
Website: www.highheelgolfer.com

John Ribeiro
Fotowurx Inc.
Website: www.fotowurx.com
Email: info@fotowurx.com

Julie Smith, Founder of the Success Through Stillness Approach and Peaceful Sleep System
Nature Meditations – Success Through Stillness
Website: www.julie-smith.net
Email: julie@julie-smith.net

Kimberly Robb Baker
Chief Career Storyteller, Movin' On Up Résumés
Website: www.movinonupresumes.com
Email: Kim@movinonupresumes.com

Lauren Holliday
Journalist, full-stack marketer
Website: http://thisisforthecrazyones.com
Email: lah@freelanship.com

LoriAnne Fitzpatrick
Director of Enterprise, Reporting & Analytics
Rogers Communications

Marguerite Orane
Marguerite Orane & Associates
Website: www.margueriteorane.com
Email: marguerite@margueriteorane.com

Maureen McCann
Chief Career Strategist & Owner
ProMotion Career Solutions
Website: www.mypromotion.ca
Email: Maureen@mypromotion.ca

Stephen Hinton
Hinton Human Capital
Website: www.hintonhumancapital.com
Email: admin@hintonhumancapital.com

Sue Edwards
Development By Design Leadership Coaching and Onboarding
Website: www.development-by-design.com
Email: info@development-by-design.com

Wayne Pagani
W. P. Consulting & Associates
Website: www.developcareers.ca
Email: developcareers@gmail.com

Razwana Wahid
Owner & Writer, Your Work Is Your Life
Website: www.yourworkisyourlife.com

About the Author

DAISY WRIGHT has gained a reputation as one of Canada's top career and employment strategists and has received several awards for her achievements. Through her company, **The Wright Career Solution**, she helps mid-career professionals, managers and executives tell their career stories and get hired FASTER!

Her corporate work experience began in Jamaica, includes a stint with UNIFEM, (now UN Women) in New York, and continued in the corporate arena in Canada. A former instructor in the Faculty of Business at Sheridan College, she honed her training and facilitation skills while teaching Business Communication and other courses to the executive administration group.

Some of Daisy's work have been published in nine of the more popular résumé, cover letter and career books. Recognized as a subject matter expert, Daisy is often contacted for career advice by Canada's national newspaper, **The Globe & Mail**, as well as the **Toronto Sun**. She is a founding member of Career Professionals of Canada, and has been honoured several times by the organization as Outstanding Canadian Career Leader.

Daisy holds a BA in Public Administration from Ryerson University, a Post-graduate Diploma in Career Development from Conestoga College and was recognized by the College with the 2011 Alumni of Distinction award.

She has been a mentor to women and internationally-trained professional students, and was nominated for a 2011 Zonta Women of Achievement award by the Brampton-Caledon Chapter of Zonta International.

Read more about Daisy at www.daisywright.com and www.thewrightcareer.com.

Made in the USA
Charleston, SC
24 March 2015